IMAGES
*of America*

# CONESUS LAKE

Map labels (hand-drawn):

LAKEVILLE

PEBBLE BEACH

CAMP RUN

RT. 20A

Town of Geneseo
219
220

3442
3440

3408
3406 DUROCHER
3308 WILKINS TRACT
3299

Boller Ave
Ely Ave
Millard Ave

CLUNY POINT

GRAYSHORES 302
304

TUXEDO PARK

GRAYWOOD 390
371

SLEGG'S LANDING 482
484

3134
3132
3067 VAN ZANDT Rd.
3066

CEDAR CREST

EAGLE POINT 513
512

DENSMORE Rd.
2944
2942

OLD ORCHARD
COVE

SACKETT'S HARBOUR
RESERVOIR Rd. 553W
554

CLEARY Rd.
2794
2792

OLD ORCHARD
POINT

WADSWORTH'S
COVE 687

PRICE Rd.

McPHERESON
COVE

LONG POINT
Long Point Rd. 762

2699
2678-E

McPHERESON
POINT

LONG POINT
COVE 753
878
880

2558
2556
2515
2513-E

HARTSON POINT

COTTONWOOD
COVE
-Boomer Rd.

HOLMES Rd.

SUNNY SHORES

1085-W
1086

2293
2291

COTTON WOOD
POINT

EXCELSIOR
SPRINGS

1283
1284

2017
2015

MAPLE BEACH

MAPLE BEACH Rd.
1700
1773

1868
1865

WALKLEY'S
LANDING

DAVID GRAY Hill Rd.
SHORES

SLIKER

HENDERSON Hill Rd.
PACOLA SHORES Rd.

CONESUS LAKE
Town of Livonia
Town of Geneseo
Town of Conesus
Town of Groveland

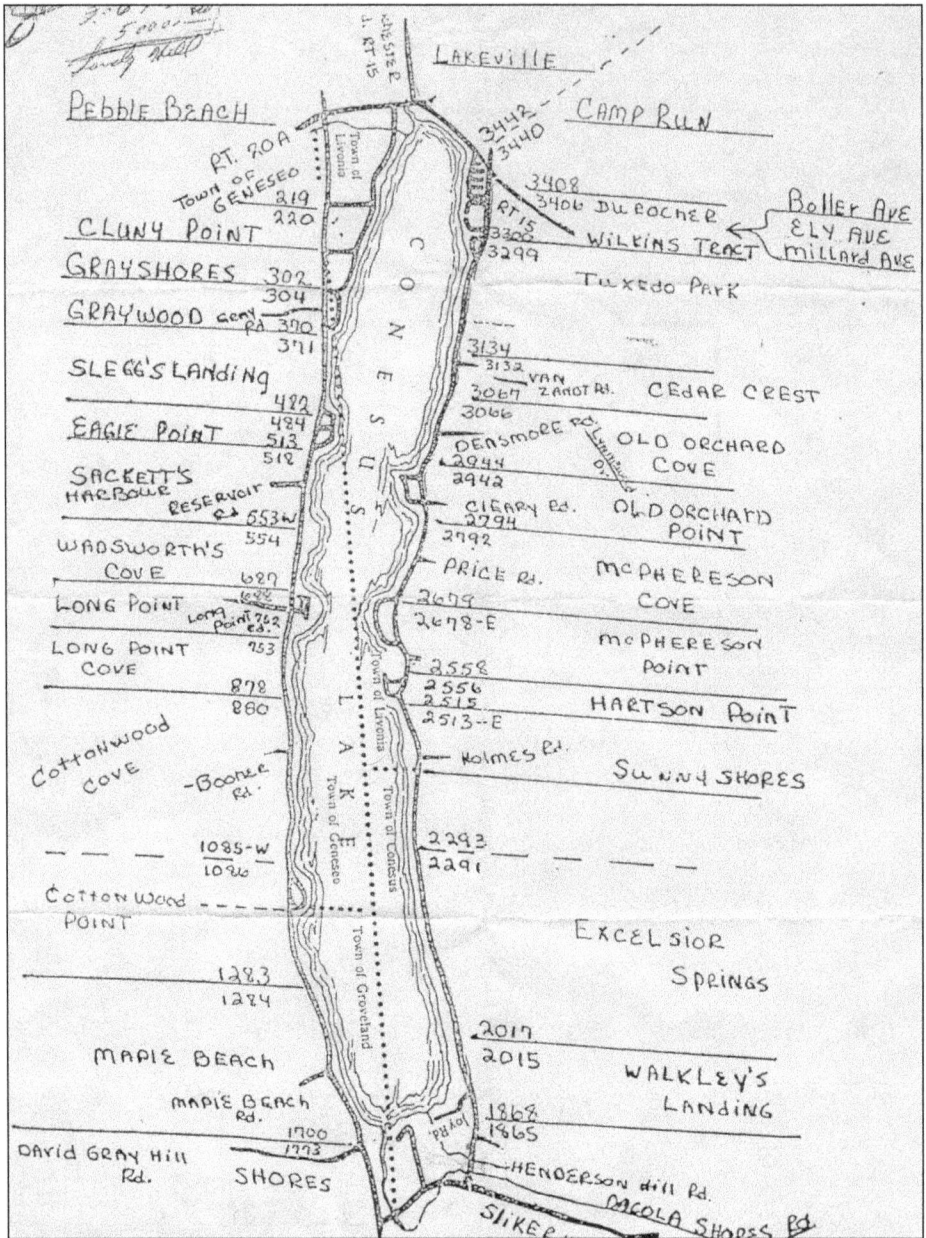

This undated map shows the borders of the four towns that line the shores of Conesus Lake. It also shows the different sections, some of which were named for early businessmen and entrepreneurs. Note that McPherson is spelled incorrectly. (Author's collection.)

ON THE COVER: The shore of Conesus Lake was a marshy, soggy area in the early years, so the docks that were built extended quite a distance out into the water. Several hotels were built on the dock that is just beyond the long, thin peninsula. The Spencer House was built in 1888 by James Henry Spencer, and the Fishermans House, owned by Bill Forman, was constructed at the same time. They catered to tourists, fishermen, and the men of the ice harvest. (Purchased from the Albert R. Stone Negative Collection, Rochester Museum and Science Center, Rochester, New York.)

IMAGES
*of America*

# CONESUS LAKE

Sharon L. Mistretta

ARCADIA
PUBLISHING

Published by Arcadia Publishing
Charleston, South Carolina

Library of Congress Control Number: 2013955781

For all general information, please contact Arcadia Publishing:
Telephone 843-853-2070
Fax 843-853-0044
E-mail sales@arcadiapublishing.com
For customer service and orders:
Toll-Free 1-888-313-2665

Visit us on the Internet at www.arcadiapublishing.com

*I dedicate this book to my husband, Richard "Dick" Mistretta, who never said a word when I disappeared into the office for days at a time to research the book, and also to my two grandsons, Donovan Julius Rodriguez and David Anthony Brongo III, whom I hope will someday gaze upon the sparkling waters of Conesus Lake and feel as much at home as I do.*

# CONTENTS

# ACKNOWLEDGMENTS

A book like this could not have been finished without the help of people behind the scenes, who talked up the project amongst the locals, pointed me in the right direction, offered me encouragement to continue when I hit a dead end, and gave me items to keep. I will keep them safe and pass them on. Thanks are given to the following: Amie Alden and her crew from the Livingston County Historian's Office; Maurice Barkley; Richard Brugnoni; Dave Headley, owner of Leisure's Restaurant; Lloyd Higbie; Inge Holling; Greg Hetzler; Anna Kowalchuk, Livingston County Historical Society Museum; Thomas and Mary Alice May, owners of the Beachcomber; Art Messinger; Norine O'Connell; David Parish, Geneseo historian; Robyn Price; Richard Meier, Rochester Gas & Electric (RG&E) public affairs; Tom Tryniski and his website *Old Fulton Postcards*; and Steve Weider. Special thanks go to Livonia historian Dorothy Wilkins. Many enjoyable afternoons were spent at the Maurice F. Sweeney Museum where I heard new-to-me stories about the area and of my grandmother and her family. Unless otherwise noted, all photographs are from my private collection.

# INTRODUCTION

The westernmost lake of the 11 Finger Lakes, Conesus has often been referred to as one of the "Little Fingers." It is located about 25 miles south of the city of Rochester in Western New York. There are four towns that border the approximate 18 miles of shoreline; they are Geneseo, in the northwest corner; Groveland, south of that town on the west side; Conesus, at the southern end; and Livonia, wrapping around the corner to the northeast. The hamlet of Lakeville is within the town of Livonia and is the only community center that still exists on the lakeshore. Two attempts were made to create a village of the hamlet, once in 1814 and again in 1822. Maps were drawn plotting out lots and streets, including a public square, all in the hopes of having Lakeville chosen as the county seat. The honor, however, was given to the nearby town of Geneseo.

According to scientific theory, 400 million years ago during the Paleozoic Era, Conesus Lake was part of an inland sea. Then as the climate changed, an ice cap was formed and then melted. These northward-receding glaciers dug into the earth with the constant push and pull of the melting ice. The deep valleys that were created filled with water and formed the Finger Lakes. The Seneca Nation, which once inhabited the Conesus Lake area, has a legend about the lakes being formed by the hand of the Great Spirit as he pressed it upon the earth.

The Native American Seneca people are the largest nation of the Six Nations of the Iroquois Confederacy in New York State. They are considered the "Keepers of the Western Door" as they are located the farthest west of all the nations in the confederacy. The Iroquois Confederacy, or Haudenosaunee, as they called themselves, encompassed the greater part of Western New York, and Seneca villages were located all over the area from Canandaigua Lake to the Genesee River centuries before European settlement. In 1779, as Sullivan's army marched across the Conesus inlet during the Revolutionary War, there were a number of long houses in a Seneca village on the east side near the head of the lake. Although the village and crops were destroyed completely, artifacts from both sides have been found in the area in years since. After the war, the news from the soldiers of the fertile fields of corn, the orchards, and timber brought many settlers to the area, including some of the men from Sullivan's army. The Treaty of Canandaigua was signed on November 11, 1794, and the Nations of the Haudenosaunee agreed to peaceful relations.

The last names of early residents can still be seen on maps and mailboxes of the towns that surround Conesus Lake. The lake itself is said to be named after a small berry that grew along the shore; the Native Americans called it Gah-nyuh-sas, meaning "Place of Many Berries." There is also a legend that it was named after a famous Indian chief.

In the town of Conesus, Henderson Hill Road runs east and west, connecting with East Lake Road near the head of the lake as it travels up a steep hill. In the late 1950s and early 1960s, motorcycle hill climbs were held on weekends at that southern corner where the two roads meet. When motorcycles were not filling the air with the noise of their engines, donkey baseball games were held between Livonia and Conesus firemen at that very same spot.

The Lindsley family originally owned land on McPherson Point on the east side. In 1881, Col. James A. McPherson bought the property at the end of the point and made it a stop for his steamboat, the *McPherson*. At the helm, making three stops a day at the point, was Capt. W.J. Keays. He had commanded a company in the 16th New York Cavalry during the Civil War. This was one of the regiments that had helped to capture John Wilkes Booth after the assassination of Pres. Abraham Lincoln. Keays was awarded a medal by Congress for his part in the capture and wore it proudly on his coat next to his Grand Army badge.

In 1814, Millard Fillmore spent some time a few miles south of Conesus Lake in Sparta, New York. He was just 14 years old when he took on an apprenticeship with Benjamin Hungerford, a cloth-maker. At first, he was sent to do menial household chores of the time, such as chopping wood, but after a stern talk with his mentor, he finished out his time learning the trade. He entered politics and became the 13th president of the United States.

The pond lilies used to grow so thick at both the inlet and the outlet of the lake that it was difficult to paddle a boat or canoe through the water. Residents Leslie Clark and William Carnes Jr. scooped them up and sold them to the tourists at Lakeville. Some of the blossoms were also sold to Rochester florists.

In 1924, the City of Rochester announced that it was undertaking the idea of using water from Conesus Lake to supplement the water supply for residents of the city. A group of engineers was formed to survey the area. Cottagers around the lake feared that using the water for public consumption might jeopardize their use of the lake as a summer resort. Hemlock had already been acquired by the city, and all cottages had been removed from that shoreline as a result. The cottagers banded together in 1925 at a meeting in the dance hall at McPherson Point. The attempt by the city was thwarted, and Conesus was spared, but meanwhile, the eyes of the city looked northward to Lake Ontario.

The lake area continued to grow, and Conesus Lake of the Little Fingers, which had reported 170 motorboats in 1910 and 700 cottages in 1925, exploded into a playground for residents and visitors alike. The music and noise of the restaurants, bars, and taverns, which lined the lakeshore, spilled into the night. The owners aimed to please, and to draw in the customers, they offered dinners, lunches, boats, bait and tackle, and even ladies to keep you company if needed. The early residents believed that if you had one drink at each establishment, you could make the drive around the lake, but if you had two drinks at each place, there was no way you would make it around.

The 1950s brought about the opening of mom-and-pop grocery stores, and the lake did not lack in a number of them. Local blue law stated that you could operate a grocery store out of your home if you had fewer than 15 employees, consisting of mostly family members, and did not conduct business on Sunday. Stores such as these could be found in all four towns around the lake. Some of the mom-and-pop stores were run by the Cavigliano, Searle, Pauer, Kulzer, Toal, and Lodico families. Toal's Grocery on the west side of the lake was well known for its "sample cheese." The store stocked huge rounds of Cuba cheese, made in Cuba, New York. The owners were more than happy to slice off a sample for customers to taste. The sharp cheddar was a favorite, and people from all over the lake would come to shop at the store.

The lake is quieter now, more of a residential area. There are only two restaurants on the water's edge, the Beachcomber, established in 1953, and the North Shore Grill in Lakeville. There are also only two grocery stores, the Shoreless Acres General Store, located on the east side, and Westlake Station, formerly Toal's, on the west side. However quiet, it is still the jewel of the Finger Lakes to the many residents and visitors who grace its shore.

# One

# CONESUS LAKE

Conesus Lake stretches north at 7.8 miles in length with the hamlet of Lakeville at its foot. The two points that come together at the shortest width are Long Point on the left and McPherson Point on the right. Just about the same time this photograph was taken, in the early 1940s, a study by the Conesus Lake Sportman's Club reported the lake's depth as 66 feet. (Courtesy of Linda Crane Culbertson.)

Conesus Inlet helps to make up the main water supply for the whole of the lake. North and South McMillan Creeks flow down from the hills at the southern end of the lake to join with waters from the inlet that in turn flow into the lake. The water does not stay long in the lake, however, as it continues on the journey north to the Genesee River and then to Lake Ontario. The average time it stays in the lake is one to three years. (Courtesy of Norman "Ron" and Nancy Anderson.)

*Aug. 30. 1906.*

*Dear Katie*

*Will see you next week.*

*Elizabeth*

Conesus Lake Inlet, Viewed From Maple Beach.

Looking south, Conesus Inlet is bordered by the town of Groveland to the west and the town of Conesus to the east. The New York State Department of Environmental Conservation first began to buy the acreage of this area in the late 1960s in order to preserve the natural habitat for fish and wildlife. Accumulating over 1,100 acres, the swampy wetland area not only preserves the spawning grounds for several types of fish but also supports a heronry for the great blue heron.

10

A member of the Rochester Automobile Club stands on the dock at the shoreline of the Excelsior Springs Hotel. The club was participating in one of their weekly auto tours from Rochester to the Dansville area with stops on the lake. In 1913, the then owner of the hotel, O.F. Leiders, advertised "Special Automobile Dinners to order, or on short notice. Phone, write or call," in order to attract their business. (Purchased from the Albert R. Stone Negative Collection, Rochester Museum and Science Center, Rochester, New York.)

Hudson River School artist John Frederick Kensett (1816–1872) painted this lake scene in 1870. He had a friend and art patron in Robert M. Olyphant, who had a residence on the lake that he visited frequently. Known as a master of luminism in American landscape painting, he has captured the peacefulness of that era in time. Titled "Summer Day at Conesus Lake," it hangs in the Metropolitan Museum of Art, New York.

As viewed from the water in 1929, here is Sutton Point. Eugene Sutton and his wife, Louise, lived in what they called the "Big House" on the left with their family. They rented out the area to the right for camping. When marital problems took their toll, Eugene simply moved out to a self-built shack on the property along with the campers. (Courtesy of Linda Crane Culbertson.)

A view of the east side of the lake from a west side farmer's pasture shows the amount of farmland that surrounded the area in the early part of the 20th century. The Livingston Inn sits on the shoreline of McPherson Point, while a boat can be seen docked at the north peninsula of Long Point just above the tree line. (Courtesy of Norman "Ron" and Nancy Anderson.)

An unidentified man stands on a patch of gravel off the northern tip of Long Point Park c. 1930s. The position of the shoreline was controlled by nature. Flooding occurred alternately with dry spells according to the change of seasons. The water level of the lake was not formally regulated until 1964. (Courtesy of Norman "Ron" and Nancy Anderson.)

The north side of McPherson Point is shown on a calm fall day in 1907. A tour boat is stopped at the dock at the end of the point. Across the lake, the slope of the toboggan ride can be seen at Long Point. (Courtesy of Norman "Ron" and Nancy Anderson.)

The roads around the lake consisted of dirt in the early 1900s and closely followed the lakeshore. In the early 1920s, only the northern end of West Lake Road had been spread with gravel, which had been provided by the bordering towns along with cottagers of Eagle Point. Long Point Hill Road was a corduroy road at this time. (Courtesy of the Village and Town of Geneseo.)

This 1940s view of Sutton Point, taken from the air, shows that the point is really not one but two small points that extend into the water. State Route 256 can be seen running alongside the western shore of the lake. The camping tents of the 1920s have disappeared and have been replaced with permanent cottages. (Courtesy of Linda Crane Culbertson.)

Temperance Beach, Conesus Lake, N. Y.

Sand Point, south of Eagle Point, became known as Temperance Beach due to the annual camp meeting of the society of the same name. The temperance movement was a social movement aimed at reducing or prohibiting the use of alcoholic beverages. Meetings were held at the point during the month of August, beginning in 1882. Interestingly, early deeds from the sale of cottages in that area show a clause that prohibits the sale of "intoxicating liquors" on the premises. (Courtesy of Norman "Ron" and Nancy Anderson.)

An unidentified man sits on a fence high above Conesus Lake in the area of Decker Road. The southern end of the McPherson Point Road can be seen on the right. Photographers were known to coax tourists into posing for a picture in areas around the lake for profit. This postcard is stamped 1903. The lakeside property behind the center tree was sold on March 25, 1960, in order to construct a public boat launch. The boat launch opened the summer of 1962. Operations were taken over by the New York State Parks Division in 1967. (Courtesy of Barb Rainer.)

15

This aerial view of Lakeville from the foot of the lake was taken in 1969. Looking north, the point on the right is now Vitale Park, owned by the Town of Livonia. Concerts are held at the park during the summer months. The area on the left is known as Pebble Beach. (Courtesy of John A. "Cubby" Rhode Jr.)

# Two

# EARLY YEARS

Maj. Gen. John Sullivan's army was instructed by Congress in 1779 to protect the frontier and settlers from Seneca Indian raids. Marching over the hills off the southeast corner of Conesus Lake, he encountered an Indian village just east of the inlet. After destroying the village and cornfields completely, he camped with his army on the same spot until a bridge could be built to cross the inlet. (Courtesy of Dorothy Ann Lush Liberati.)

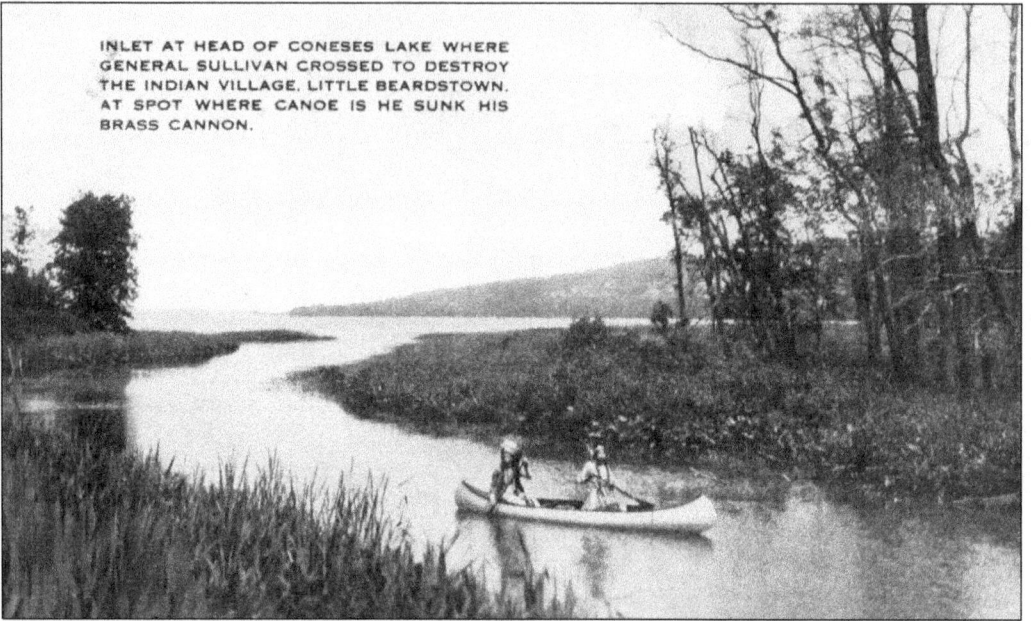

INLET AT HEAD OF CONESES LAKE WHERE
GENERAL SULLIVAN CROSSED TO DESTROY
THE INDIAN VILLAGE, LITTLE BEARDSTOWN.
AT SPOT WHERE CANOE IS HE SUNK HIS
BRASS CANNON.

In order for Sullivan to cross the muddy inlet with the thousands of men and horses that made up his army, logs were placed side by side to form a corduroy bridge. The exact location is not known, but records state that it was supposed to have been two-thirds of a mile long. Historians do know, however, that no cannon sunk in the inlet.

This 1956 view of Sliker Hill Road, seen heading west at the southern end of the lake, is part of the route that Major General Sullivan took with his army in search of a great Seneca town on the Genesee River. It is from this area that he sent Lt. Thomas Boyd and Sgt. Michael Parker on a scouting party. Traveling at night, the party actually passed a group of Indians from the town in the darkness without knowing the presence of each other. (Courtesy of the Livingston County Historians Office.)

18

This narrow trail follows a ridge near the head of Conesus Lake. Reported as part of an old Indian trail by the *Rochester Herald* of June 1915, it follows the top of what is known as an esker. An esker is a geological term used to define the long winding ridge formed by the flow of a retreating glacier. (Purchased from the Albert R. Stone Negative Collection, Rochester Museum and Science Center, Rochester, New York.)

Old Log Cabin at Head of Conesus Lake erected in 1779 on Site of Indian Village destroyed by General Sullivan.

After Major General Sullivan had destroyed the Indian town and cornfields at the head of the lake, pioneer settlers took over the area and built their own log cabins. Several journals of Sullivan's officers speak of the fertility of the land, the extensive cornfields, vegetable fields, and the heavy forests of timber. Some soldiers were so impressed with the surrounding area that they returned after the war to raise a family and begin settlement.

Arrowheads such as these have been found all over the Finger Lakes region, usually near lakes and rivers where Native Americans hunted and fished. As the home of the Seneca Indian Nation, arrowheads have been discovered all around Conesus Lake. In this c. 1916 photograph, the arrowhead to the far right was found at Conesus. They have also been found as recent as 1984 at a new home construction site on the lake. (Purchased from the Albert R. Stone Negative Collection, Rochester Museum and Science Center, Rochester, New York.)

This area at the southern end of East Lake Road is the site of the first mill built by James Henderson, a settler from Pennsylvania. He was a millwright by trade and came to the town of Conesus, along with his wife and children, in 1793. In 1816, he built the first woolen and fulling mill in a gully at the head of Conesus Lake. (Courtesy of the Livingston County Historians Office.)

The McMillan Homestead at the head of Conesus Lake was built in the same area of the first Henderson mill. The house was the residence of R.F. and B.F. McMillan in 1872, descendants of the Henderson family. Another family member, Charles McMillan, was US minister to China in 1881. (Courtesy of the Livingston County Historians Office.)

A.W. Butterways was a cabinetmaker and owner of a successful furniture business in 1850 in Geneseo, New York. In addition to his store on Main Street and his home on Second Street in Geneseo, he built this cottage on West Lake Road in Groveland about 1880. (Courtesy of the Livingston County Historians Office.)

An unidentified man is standing in front of an early cabin on Conesus Lake. The photograph is dated 1915, but the location of the cabin is unknown. (Courtesy of the Village and Town of Geneseo.)

A small village developed at the head of the lake around the inlet after James Henderson first settled here in 1793. There were four taverns, a blacksmith, and the Pridmore Hotel among the half-dozen houses that made up the village. J.G. Pridmore, owner and proprietor of the hotel, is pictured in front leading the cow. The hotel burned in 1881 under his ownership. Also pictured are Mrs. J.G. Pridmore, at right of cow; Mrs. John Van Valkenburg, back of cow; Sarah Pridmore (later Mrs. John Finnegan), on upstairs porch at front; and Mary Pridmore (later Mrs. Thomas Allen), on upstairs porch at right. There is not a trace today of the hotel or the village. (Courtesy of the Livingston County Historians Office)

Life for early residents was one of survival, and the lake provided them with plenty of places to hunt and fish. This unidentified man is holding the bounty of his hunt around 1915. He is standing on a corduroy road at an unknown location around the lake. (Courtesy of the Village and Town of Geneseo.)

This cottage on McPherson Point, pictured around 1892, was called Elmwood. Among the cottagers relaxing around the porch are J.C. Wilson, his wife, their two girls, and one boy; Mrs. Hixson and her three children; and Mr. and Mrs. Shaw. (Courtesy of the Livingston County Historians Office.)

The Burger family purchased land from George Hanna in 1909. John Burger, a potter, of Rochester, New York, built two houses on the property. This cottage was built for Emma Burger Penton and called Pleasant View. The other was built for her sister-in-law Hattie E. Burger. The family would drive from Rochester to the Lakeville pier and take a steamboat to the cottage; they had to walk to Lakeville to get their mail. (Courtesy of Jean Stauber Taylor.)

The tradition of naming a cottage was carried on long after summer cottages turned into year-around homes. Acirema, the house seen above, is America spelled backwards. The sign hung on the cottage of Fred Schaller just two doors south of this location in the 1960s. Handed down to his daughter, it was finally removed in July 2013, after more than 50 years on display.

School commissioners organized McMillan District No. 2 Schoolhouse on March 17, 1823. It was called McMillan District after the family that first settled the area at the head of the lake. The last teacher at the schoolhouse was Florence Joy; the school district then was merged into the Livonia Central School System after more than 115 years of service. (Courtesy of the Livingston County Historians Office.)

The McMillan District No. 2 class of October 1939 is pictured. Students are, from left to right, (first row) Betty Thomas, Barton Jacobs, and Bruce Barber; (second row) Bernard Seeley, Marilyn Seeley, Ernest Rowe, Harry Rowe, William Seeley, and James Barber; (third row) Dorothy Giltner, Mary Dale, Kenneth Giltner, and teacher Florence Joy. (Courtesy of the Livingston County Historians Office.)

The Pennemite District schoolhouse was established in 1841. It sat on a hill above the lake at the Cedar Crest section and was officially known as District No. 3. In 1842, teacher Ormiel Bigelow was paid $15 dollars per month. The students were blended into the Livonia High School in 1939 when centralization of districts took place. That year, the schoolhouse and property sold for $100. (Courtesy of the Donald and Bernice Wolf Collection.)

An unidentified farmhand feeds the chickens in the yard of Sunnyside farm, owned by Harper Day. On Sunday afternoons in the summer, the farm was opened up to cottagers and area residents alike in order to hold a vesper religious service. There was music, and sermons were given on the lawn. (Courtesy of Mary Lee Cisco.)

Farm employees from the Harper Day farm maneuver a team of oxen down East Lake Road. The road was dirt, carved from nothing more than a horse trail. Residents of the southern end of the lake road were still waiting for electricity in October 1923, as the power lines stopped halfway down the lake just south of McPherson Point. (Courtesy of Mary Lee Cisco.)

Scene at _____
Cave of the Owls in Glen of Glenacker
Supposed to be a Bear Den in early times.

Harold Acker (left) and Marion Acker (right) are sitting at the entrance to a cave near the hamlet of Glenacker around 1900. Vineyards and a wine cellar run by F.M. Acker were located at the hamlet at the southern end of East Lake Road. The small village had a post office, and Capt. Dan Walkley served as postmaster in 1905. (Courtesy of Norman "Ron" and Nancy Anderson.)

In 1908, Samuel T. Jennings wrote this Conesus Lake love song, "Dear Conesus Lake," with music by Lee Carleton. (Courtesy of Maureen Reynolds.)

# DEAR CONESUS LAKE

SAMUEL T. JENNINGS.

LEE CARLETON.

Copyright MCMVIII by Samuel T. Jennings, Genesco, N.Y.

Samuel T. Jennings, who was a teacher by trade, graduated from the State Normal and Training School at Geneseo in 1893. (Courtesy of Maureen Reynolds.)

boat was drift - ing id - ly thro' the rip - ples, Which
failed to un - der - stand the love I told you, You

seem'd to dance in glad-ness for your sake, My heart was thrill'd with love's di - vin - est
thought I said it on - ly to de-ceive, You left me and my heart was filled with

pas - sion, That night we spent at dear Co - ne - sus Lake.
sad - ness, My life my hope my fu - ture I did leave.

**Chorus Tempo di Valse**

At Co - ne-sus that beau - ti - ful Lake ____ The best pic -tures that na-ture could

*Dear Conesu Lake . 3 . 2*

Jennings, who lived in Geneseo, would go on to become editor of the *Livingston Republican* newspaper during the 1930s. (Courtesy of Maureen Reynolds.)

make, ____ Were pre - sent - ed to view And I swear it was true That I thought it was all for your sake, ____ The dark trees that stood by the shore, And the soft star-light (lit) sky spreading o'er ____ Filled my heart with de-light, And I loved you that night As maid-en was ne'er loved be fore. ____

Lee Carleton, who wrote the musical score to Jennings lyrics, also wrote music for several songs from that period in time. The song by Jennings and Carleton can be found in its entirety on file at the Milne Library, in the State University of Geneseo, at Geneseo, New York. (Courtesy of Maureen Reynolds.)

The *Jessie* was the first steamboat on the lake. Owner Jerry Bolles was also the proprietor of the Lake View House, the first hotel on the lake. The steamer was launched from the dock at the hotel on July 1, 1874. Beam's Canadice band and the old-time band from Richmond played at the celebration to a crowd of 5,000 onlookers. (Courtesy of the Livingston County Historians Office.)

The *Erminie* was a steam launch that raced in regattas held on the lake in the late 1800s. In an 1888 edition, the *Rochester Democrat and Chronicle* advertised a regatta on Conesus Lake with special train excursions to view the race. The cost from Rochester to the lake was 75¢ round-trip. The *Erminie* won the steam launch division in 1898. (Courtesy of the Livingston County Historians Office.)

The steamboat *McPherson* made daily stops at the Long Point dock to drop off park visitors as well as local cottage residents. Named after Col. James A. McPherson, who had it built in Lakeville in the early 1880s, it was the largest and most famous ship that ran on Conesus Lake. It had three decks that could hold 1,000 passengers, a dance floor, and a refreshment bar. (Courtesy of Walter Kingston Jr., Long Point Museum and Information Center.)

Daniel Clarke Walkey, known as Captain Dan, ran steamers on the lake for 36 years. The *White Swan* was brought from Hemlock Lake in 1887 in order to deliver provisions and passengers on Conesus Lake. F. Acker of Lakeville and C.S. Dewey of Maple Beach owned it. (Courtesy of Norman "Ron" and Nancy Anderson.)

The double-decker *Conesus* was launched the summer of 1903. Owned by Walter Strowger, who, at the time, was the owner of the Livingston Inn, *Conesus* would take guests of the inn on after-dinner cruises around the lake. There was usually a band, and the decks were cleared for dancing, especially square dancing. Equipped with a 75-horsepower engine, it was the fastest boat on the lake. (Courtesy of Walter Kingston Jr., Long Point Museum and Information Center.)

The *Jaegar* and the *Alice M.* were the first two boats acquired by the D.C. Walkley Transportation Company. Formed in the early 1900s, the company owned four boats. The boats had scheduled trips to meet the commuter trains in Lakeville, and when time permitted, they took passengers on excursion trips around the lake. The *Alice M.* was the designated boat for the west side of the lake. (Courtesy of the Livingston County Historians Office.)

A.W. Springstead of Geneva built the *J.A. Ritz*, named after cottager Jacob A. Ritz, of the *Rochester and Union Advertiser* newspaper, in 1906. By 1918, transportation by steamboat had waned, and the *Ritz* met its demise. The steamboat was cut up for timber with the bow becoming a pigpen at the home of its captain, Dan Walkley. (Courtesy of Dorothy Ann Lush Liberati.)

The *Rochester* is tied to the dock at Long Point while the *Ritz* steams away with a load of passengers. M.E. Durkee built the *Rochester* at Old Orchard Point on the east side in 1908. It was a gasoline-powered boat and the last of the four boats of the Capt. Dan Walkley fleet. (Courtesy of Walter Kingston Jr., Long Point Museum and Information Center.)

# *Three*

# CAMPS AND CLUBS

Pictured in 1927 are, from left to right, Gerald Lambert, Thomas Brennan, Eugene Hudson, and Joseph McDonnell. Both friends and seminarians studying for the priesthood, Gerald and Eugene founded Camp Stella Maris for Rochester's Catholic boys in 1926, with just $20 between them. The first camp was held on McPherson Point with 12 campers enrolled, and Gerald's mother was cook and camp mother. (Courtesy of John Quinlivan, Camp Stella Maris.)

Founder Gerald Lambert, who, by this time, had become Monsignor Lambert, hired Joe Morsch as caretaker in April 1947. Morsch would remain as such until 1984. Housed on the property in what is now known as the Day Camp Building, he had raised cows on what is now the playground. So well liked was this maintenance man that, in the early 1970s, a cabin was erected at the camp and named Morsch Cabin in his honor. (Courtesy John Quinlivan, Camp Stella Maris.)

Pictured is the winter camp at Camp Stella Maris in 1979. The camp was held during students' winter break from school, and as stated in that year's annual report, it provided "a Christian camping experience for children and their parents in a winter setting." (Courtesy of John Quinlivan, Camp Stella Maris.)

Staff members of Camp Stella Maris gather on the steps of the Big House in 1930. The building was originally the Lake View House, one of the first hotels built on Conesus Lake and owned and operated by Jerry Bolles at the Jerry Bolles Resort. Max Russer, who was the owner in 1927, gifted the land to the Catholic Diocese of Rochester, New York, for a permanent location. The camp used this building until 2006. (Courtesy of John Quinlivan, Camp Stella Maris.)

George Vogt stands with the first girl campers at Camp Stella Maris, located on East Lake Road, Livonia, New York, in 1939. Previously just for boys, girls from the St. Patrick's Home were allowed to come to the camp during the first week of September 1938. The first two-week regular session summer camp for girls was held in 1941. (Courtesy of John Quinlivan, Camp Stella Maris.)

Camp Rice, a Girl Scout Camp, opened in September 1949 on West Lake Road. Edward Rice, a Geneseo businessman, presented the land to them specifically for use by the Scouts. From left to right are (first row) Mary ?, Elaine Scondras, Dixie Britton, Carolyn Jamieson, and Marcia Manley; (second row) Rhea Pecora; (third row) Diane Archer, Polly Newton, Norine Vienna, Ann Megathlin, and Donna Linfoot. (Courtesy of Polly Camp.)

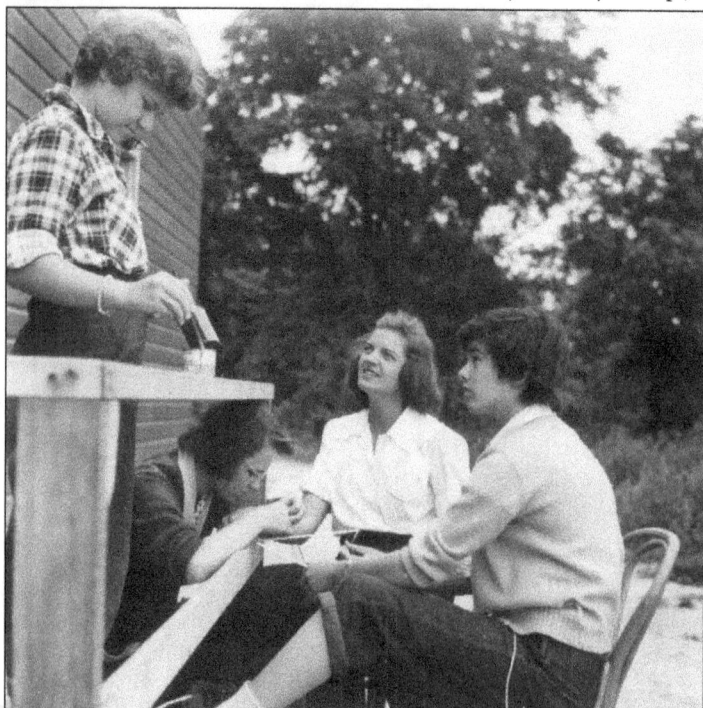

The first few years of the camp were quite rustic, with an outdoor latrine and only two platforms for tents. Initially a day camp, solicitors canvassed the area, and $4,000 was raised for improvements and equipment for overnight camping. Campers are, from left to right, Elaine Scondras, Norine Vienna, Mary Jane Linton, and Lee McBride. (Courtesy of Polly Camp.)

In addition to learning outdoor skills, such as building a campfire, the Scouts at Camp Rice cooked all their own meals. Pictured are, from left to right, unidentified, Lee McBride, Elaine Scondras, and Mary ? (Elaine's cousin). (Courtesy of Polly Camp.)

HOLIDAY HOUSE, CONESUS LAKE, GENESEO, NEW YORK

The Holiday House was a camp for the Girls Friendly Society of the Episcopal Church. Built around 1895 by the Chapin family of Rochester, New York, it was one of two houses on the lake that had a bathroom. The church purchased it in 1920, and today, it is a private residence. (Courtesy of the Livingston County Historians Office.)

INTERIOR OF CHAPEL OF GIRLS FRIENDLY HOLIDAY HOUSE, CONESUS LAKE, GENESEO, N.Y.

Atwater Memorial Chapel was built on the Holiday House property around 1928. St. Michael's Episcopal Church of Geneseo held the Sunday service for girls of the camp as well as lake residents, many of whom came by boat. Although the Episcopal Church owned it, all denominations were welcome. (Courtesy of the Livingston County Historians Office.)

Wilhelm Baumann was born in Rochester, New York, on September 4, 1884. He was an American professional wrestler and promoter. He took the American first name of William and eventually changed his entire name to Billy Sandow, a ring name. He is pictured here about 1904. Sandow operated a training camp just south of Hartson Point on East Lake Road during the 1920s and 1930s. (Courtesy of Richard Baumann.)

The Gold Dust Trio was a group of promoters that changed the course of wrestling in the early 1920s. Pictured are, from left to right, Ed "Strangler" Lewis and Billy Sandow, two-thirds of the Gold Dust Trio. Together with the third member, Joseph "Toots" Mondt, they dominated professional wrestling in the 1920s by creating the Slam Bang Wrestling style, which is essentially the World Wrestling Entertainment of today. Both Lewis and Sandow trained at the camp on Conesus Lake. (Courtesy of Richard Baumann.)

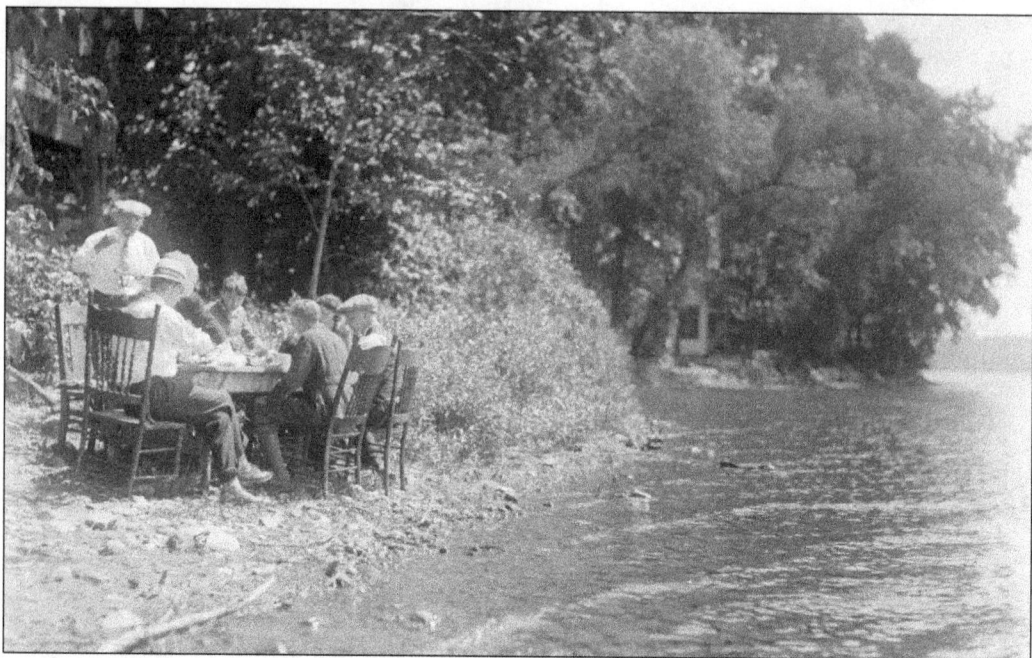

George W. Henner, standing, is enjoying a picnic with unidentified members of the Automobile Club of Rochester around 1925. The group was on a tour to the Jackson Health Resort in Dansville, stopping at the lake for an impromptu picnic. (Purchased from the Albert R. Stone Negative Collection, Rochester Museum and Science Center, Rochester, New York.)

The *Rochester Herald* newspaper sponsored auto tours together with the Automobile Club of Rochester. Standing on the dock at the Livingston Inn are, from left to right, unidentified, Miles Woodruff, unidentified, Kathryn Woodruff, and two unidentified people. The Woodruffs were proprietors of the inn. The club members were participating in the Bristol Valley Tour in 1919. (Purchased from the Albert R. Stone Negative Collection, Rochester Museum and Science Center, Rochester, New York.)

The Williamsville Rotary Club sponsored a six-week camp for boys at Long Point Park. It was held during the summer months in the mid-1920s with all of the tents, mess hall, and boating instruction provided by the club. The camp was named after Lynne Buckingham, the senior director of the Young Men's Club of Williamsville, New York. (Courtesy of Norman "Ron" and Nancy Anderson.)

Old Orchard Point was the scene of more than a few picnics for local organizations. The Livingston County American Legion Auxiliary picnic drew over 100 members in 1931. The Free Masons of Lima, New York, held their gathering in 1916 at the point, including tours by Capt. Dan Walkley on the *J.A. Ritz*. (Courtesy of Norman "Ron" and Nancy Anderson.)

The Conesus Lake Yacht Club has evolved over the years. An early gathering of yacht owners formed the yacht club in August 1895 with J.A. Ritz in charge of its meetings. The group's first regatta was held off McPherson Point that same year. Then, in 1937, another group of sailors reestablished the club at a dinner meeting held at the Tooey showroom on Long Point.

This compact was given to the lady sailors of the Conesus Lake Yacht club. The compacts were handed out at a dinner that was held at the end of the sailing and racing season. There is still a bit of red cream rouge left in one of the inside compartments. (Courtesy of Walter Kingston Jr., Long Point Museum and Information Center.)

These Comet sailboats are getting ready for weekend races at the dock of resident Morris Minor. All races were guided by the regulations of the Comet Class Yacht Racing Association, and trophies were awarded to the winners. The Comet class was a busy part of the Conesus Lake Yacht Club, and on some weekends, over two dozen were entered in the regatta. (Courtesy of Walter Kingston Jr., Long Point Museum and Information Center.)

Graywoods Campground in the summer of 1908 was filled with tents. The campers in the center are, from left to right, unidentified, Fred O'Conner, Maude Wiard, Jimmie Cadien, and Fanny Wiard. The tents in the first row belong to the Huntoon family, Netta Clark, and the Atwater family. (Courtesy of the Livingston County Historians Office.)

Passengers are unloading from the *H.T. Jaeger* at Graywoods dock around 1910. The town of Geneseo on the west side of the lake was popular for camping. Families would set up their tents and stay for weeks at a time, entertaining family members and guests throughout the summer season. (Courtesy of the Livingston County Historians Office.)

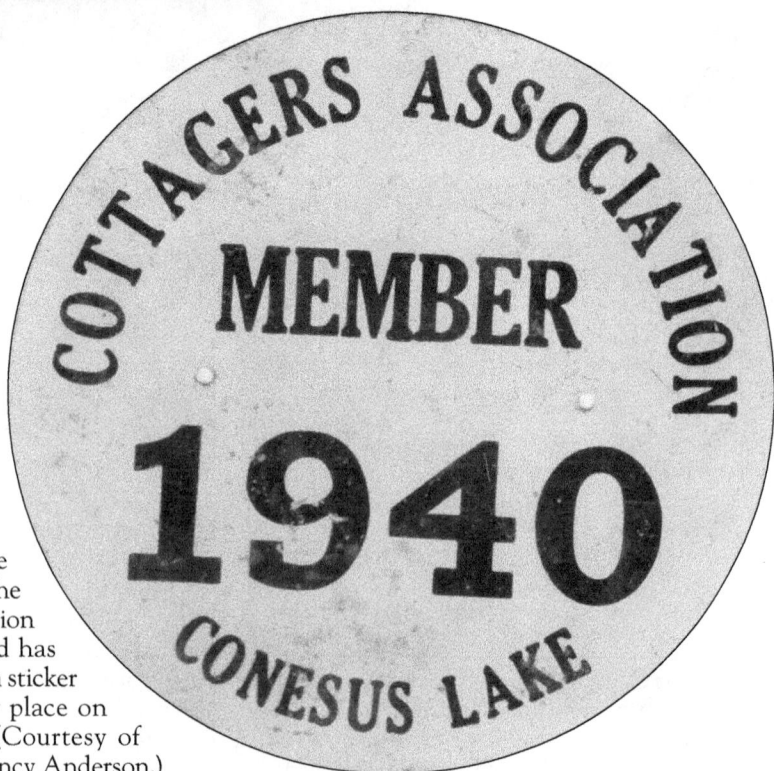

Metal shields, such as these, were given to members of the Cottagers Association of Conesus Lake. Before the days of vinyl siding, most residents nailed them to the side of the cottage or garage. The name was changed to the Conesus Lake Association about 1953. The shield has since been changed to a sticker that members proudly place on windows and doors. (Courtesy of Norman "Ron" and Nancy Anderson.)

The Conesus Lake Water Ski Club was formed at a meeting held at the Beachcomber Restaurant in July 1955. Local residents Edward and June Dickinson were instrumental in the organization of the club. These unidentified members are suited up for the 1976 US bicentennial celebration that was held around the lake. That year, the club performed stunts that included barefoot skiers, torch skiers, and this pyramid of skiers. (Courtesy of the Village and Town of Geneseo.)

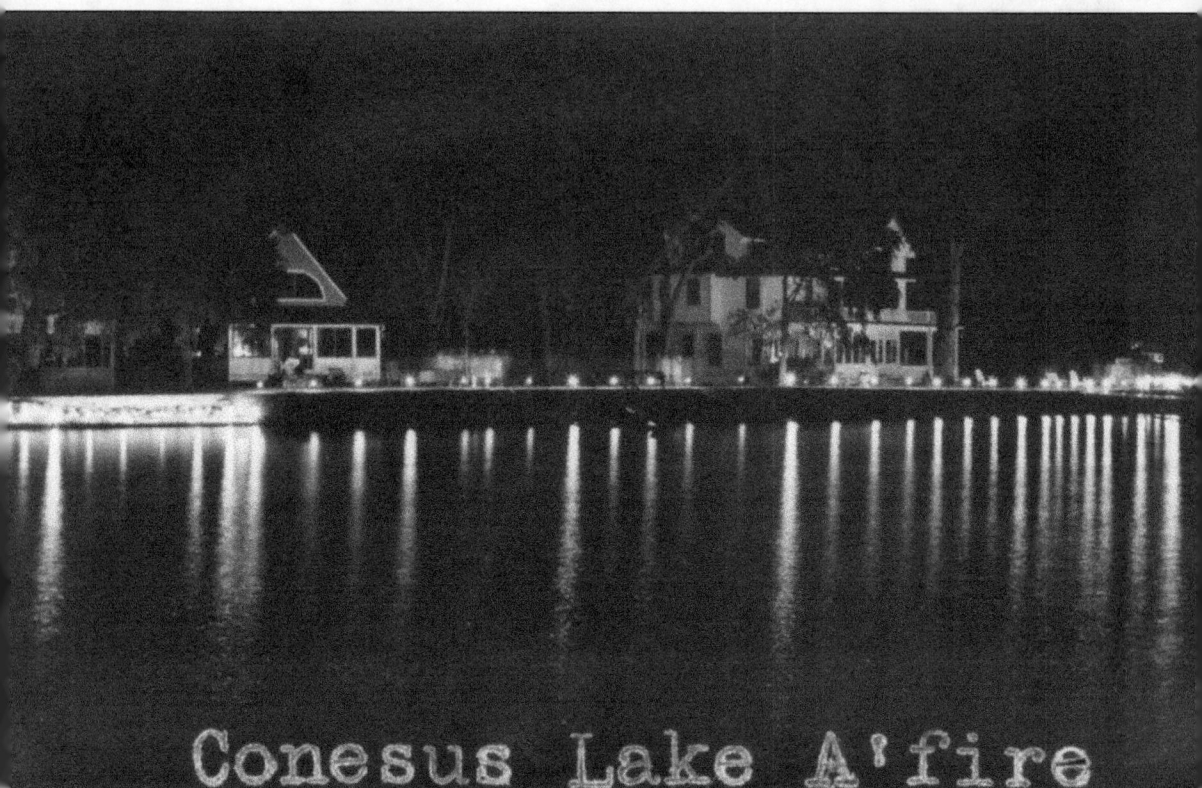

## Conesus Lake A'fire

The Lake of Fire was held for the first time on the Fourth of July in 1938. Each member of the Cottagers Association was given two road flares to set up in front of his or her cottage that were lit to form a ring around the lake. Except for a few years during and after World War II and a date change to July 3, lake residents have celebrated this every year. (Courtesy of the Livingston County Historians Office.)

# *Four*

# PEOPLE

June 1915

*Cora Nelson, Elva Burger + Mildred*

From left to right are Cora Nelson and cousins Elva Burger and Mildred Burger; they are shown with the sheep from the Hanna Farm in the area that is now known as Pebble Beach. Farmland surrounded the lake in the early part of the 20th century, which meant animals could wander down the hill to the water's edge for a drink. (Courtesy of Jean Stauber Taylor.)

Elva Burger is seen picking strawberries in Cluny Woods around 1917. The woods bordered the northwest corner of the lake, where Col. James A. McPherson built the first cottage, called Cluny Castle. There were no roads to the water at this time, so access to the lake was by foot through the sheep pasture and over the hill of the Hanna Farm. (Courtesy of Jean Stauber Taylor.)

John Burger shows off his catch from Conesus Lake while visiting family at their Pleasant View cottage. John is the grandson of potter John Burger, known for his stoneware pottery made in Rochester, New York. John was considered a most skillful potter and artistic decorator who had a special talent for shading colors. (Courtesy of Jean Stauber Taylor.)

Pictured are, from left to right, (first row)
Isaac Milton VanZandt; Lucy Wheelan, his
mother-in-law; and Stella VanZandt, his
wife; (second row) Isaac and Stella's four
children. Isaac was a prominent farmer in
the town of Livonia and, at one time, owned
190 acres above the northeastern corner of
Conesus Lake. Eventually, the road that ran
through his property took his last name.

Charles A. Williams was a photographer who
lived on McPherson Point in the early 1900s.
He loved the Old West culture so much so
that he dressed up in Western clothes and
even went by the name "Mountain Pete." He
would photograph his wife, who was of Seneca
Indian heritage, in full costume around the
lake area, using the pictures for postcards.

Photographed around 1930, Charles Williams holds a mighty string of perch on a dock at McPherson Point. There was a large population of yellow perch in the lake that attracted fishermen, especially ice fishermen. In 1974, an unofficial survey calculated that 78,000 hours of ice fishing had been done on Conesus Lake. Later, in the 1980s, the large number of yellow perch disappeared. A study by the Department of Environmental Conservation showed that a small fish called an alewive had found its way into the lake waters and ate the food and the larvae of the yellow perch, taking over its habitat.

Myrtle Sutton Williams and an unidentified man pose for the camera of Charles Williams at Conesus Inlet. Her mother, Louise, was of Seneca heritage, and her father, Eugene, was half Seneca. She very much embraced her heritage and became a most willing subject for Charles's camera, dressing in full Native American costume for his pictures. She died at a young age in April 1926.

Myrtle Sutton is photographed in her Native American costume. She lived in the town of Groveland on the west side of the lake with her family in 1910. She made newspaper headlines when she saved two fishermen from drowning off Cottonwood Point using her own leaky rowboat to bring them to shore. The point where she lived was renamed Sutton Point in her honor.

## Plucky Indian Maid Saves 2 from Drowning

### Conesus Lake Cottagers Think Myrtle Sutton Should Have Carnegie Medal for Her Heroism.

Two members of the Conesus Lake cottage colony, both men, owe their lives to the courage and presence of mind of a Seneca Indian girl, Miss Myrtle Sutton, who saved them from drowning in an accident off Cotton-

—Photo by Chas. Williams.
Miss Myrtle Sutton.

wood point one evening last week. Cottagers who witnessed the rescue are unanimous in the declaration that it was daring enough to merit consideration by the Carnegie medal fund.

Miss Sutton, who lives with her parents on Iroquois Point, was gazing out over the water about dusk when she noticed an overturned boat, with a man clinging desperately to its bottom while another paddled alongside, giving it headway enough to keep it from sinking. Without waiting to call for help, Miss Sutton dashed down to the dock and into a rowboat, which she rowed out to the scene. Her own boat was leaky and water was lapping her ankles when she reached the craft on to which the two men were clinging.

One of them, it appears, had been seized with cramps and was helpless. He was unable to climb into Miss Sutton's boat and the girl was compelled to drag him in over the stern, a difficult task in view that he weighs more than 200 pounds. He was unconscious before the boat reached the dock.

Miss Sutton's father, summoned by her shouts, commandeered another boat and aided her in rescuing the second man, who had been clinging to the overturned craft. A fifty-pound weight was attached to it, making it unable to bear the entire weight of both men. The men, who had been fishing off the point until a sudden movement tipped over their boat, were cared for at the Sutton cottage until they were able to leave.

This is the newspaper article that was published telling of Myrtle Sutton's daring rescue and recommending her for a Carnegie Medal.

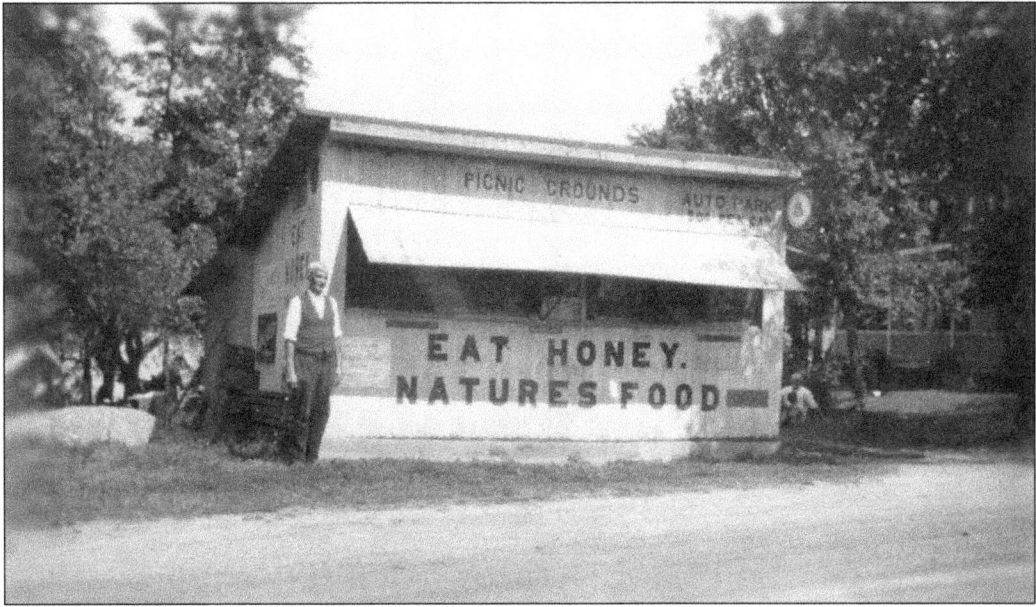

Eugene Sutton is standing next to his roadside stand on Sutton Point around 1929. He was convinced that honey was nature's perfect food and spoke of its advantages to anyone who would listen. He told his customers how honey never spoiled and that he considered it nature's natural antibiotic, himself taking one daily teaspoon. (Courtesy of Linda Crane Culbertson.)

Bess O'Connor, seen at center with the white headband, is swimming with her unidentified pals from the Normal School in Geneseo, New York, about 1900. The students are posing on the shoreline near the family cottage, located at 903 West Lake Road. They are all smiles due to their recent graduation from the school. (Courtesy of Nancy Gallagher Monahan.)

Cooling off in the water are, from left to right, Nancy Gallagher, Joan Hunt, and Sally Blatz. During the summer of 1949, the hottest day of the year fell on August 9. The temperature recorded at the nearby weather station, located at the Dansville Municipal Airport, was 95 degrees. (Courtesy of Nancy Gallagher Monahan.)

J. Fred Chichester, called "Chi" by his friends, display's the day's catch in front of his tent on Sutton Point. The campers welcomed Eugene Sutton, owner of the camp, as he taught them how to fry their fish. Later in the evening, at their campfire, he told ghost stories about an Indian in a canoe so vividly that the campers could almost see him out there on the water. (Courtesy of Linda Crane Culbertson.)

Sitting in front of the Gallagher family cottage in July 1940 are, from left to right, Mary Gallagher, daughter Nancy Gallagher, Mary Corris, and daughter Ann Corris. Mary's husband, Bob Corris, would go on to open the Beachcomber Restaurant south of the cottage in 1953. (Courtesy of Nancy Gallagher Monahan.)

Martha Welch is proud of her catch of a northern pike caught at Conesus Lake in July 1943. (Courtesy of Nancy Gallagher Monahan.)

Sitting on the porch of the Lauderdale cottage in 1904 are, from left to right, Lew O'Connor and his wife, Bess. Dr. Walter E. Lauderdale practiced medicine in Geneseo for 50 years. He held meetings of the County Medical Society at his lakeside cottage. (Courtesy of Nancy Gallagher Monahan.)

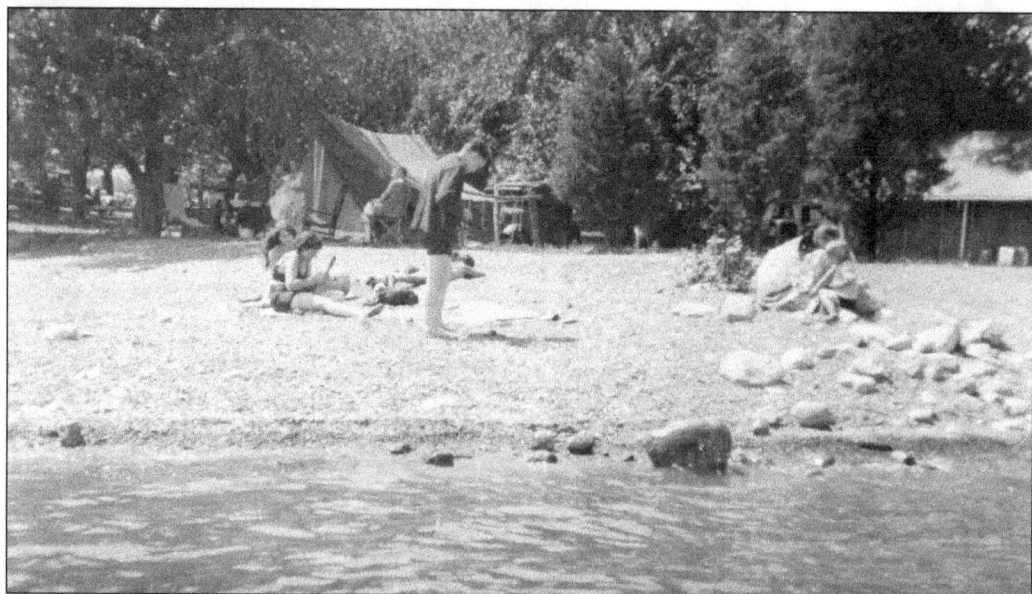

These unidentified members of the "Sutton Point Gang" are enjoying the beach at Sutton Point in the 1930s. The community water pump can be seen behind the group in front of the center cottage. All the campers took responsibility to keep the pump in good working order. This was their water supply. They did not take more than what was needed, kept the cloth that covered the spout clean, and never left the pump running. (Courtesy of Linda Crane Culbertson.)

Robert Jones Jr., age 11 months, is getting a bath while his family camps on Sutton Point. (Courtesy of Linda Crane Culbertson.)

Standing are, from left to right, Roberts Jones Sr., holding Robert Jones Jr., and Joseph Fred Chichester at their camp on Sutton Point in 1932. The two men were coworkers at Sonyea, New York, who camped with their families on the point. They both bought parcels on the property and built cottages together in the 1940s. (Courtesy of Linda Crane Culbertson.)

Otto Binder worked as a carpenter in Sonyea and was a friend of Robert Jones Sr., who owned waterfront property at Sutton Point. In this 1940s photograph, he is using a spud to break a hole through the ice. Before the invention of the ice auger, fishermen used this device to make a hole in the ice in order to set up for fishing. (Courtesy of Linda Crane Culbertson.)

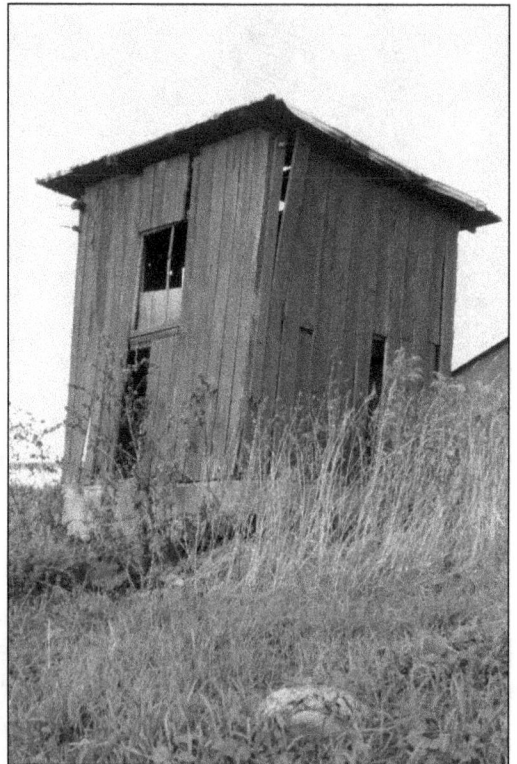

The outhouse was the only choice for most early Conesus Lake residents. This one used to sit next to a farmhouse on the east side of the lake at the corner of Cleary Road. The completion of a perimeter sewer system around the lake in 1972 helped to correct any negative environmental effects created by these such buildings. It had not seen any use for quite some time and was torn down shortly after this picture was taken in 1989.

Colonel Tooey ran a ferry service every Sunday morning to take people from the west side to St. Margaret's Catholic Church on the east side. He charged 10¢ a ride. Usually, there were so many people waiting that the line ran the full length of the Long Point dock. After the last person boarded the boat, Dick Waldeis would don his flippers and snorkel to dive for the dimes that had slipped from waiting fingers. From left to right are Carol Waldeis, Dick Waldeis, Sandy Waldeis, and Norman "Ron" Anderson. (Courtesy of Norman "Ron" and Nancy Anderson.)

Although there were concerns in the 1980s by the New York State Department of Environmental Conservation over the decline of the yellow perch and walleye populations in Conesus Lake, this 1987 photograph shows largemouth bass fishing was superb. Dave Brongo Jr. holds his catch of two largemouth taken from the east side. The lunker on his left weighed over six pounds.

Long Point Park was a favorite place of both the Livingston County Republican and Democratic political parties to hold their annual rallies. Large crowds gathered, numbering between 4,000 and 5,000 spectators. Gordon Crane, of Scottsburg, is ready to go to the Republican rally of 1936 with a team belonging to his father, Laverne Crane. (Courtesy of Linda Crane Culbertson.)

Surprised by the camera are, from left to right, Adeline "Lena" Cooligan and her aunt, Ethyl Matthews Cooligan, as they wait for their ride on the lake aboard the *J.A. Ritz*. The *Ritz* was the designated steamboat for the east side of the lake. The Cooligan family has had ancestral roots in the Lakeville area from the early 19th century to present day. (Courtesy of Dorothy Ann Lush Liberati.)

Chet Cooligan of Lakeville (left) with an unidentified member of the crew (right) is showing off his catch from a fishing charter on the *J.A. Ritz* in this undated photograph. The captain of the *Ritz* was Dan Walkley, the engineer was Leo Stark, and the deckhand was Ted Ogden. (Courtesy of Dorothy Ann Lush Liberati.)

Ida (Bennett) Day and Harper R. Day, her husband, are seen here in 1920. In the early 1900s, the couple owned Sunnyside farm on the east side of the lake in the town of Conesus. Eventually, in the 1970s, the farmland would become home to Southern Shores Campground, as it is today. (Courtesy of Mary Lee Cisco.)

Standing are, from left to right, Elizabeth Struble and Ida Day. Elizabeth helped Ida with chores at the farmhouse and with the daily care of her son. The farm had a number of beehives, and the Days grew fruits and vegetables that made their way to markets in Rochester, New York. (Courtesy of Mary Lee Cisco.)

Two generations of the Woodruff family were managers of the Livingston Inn. Sitting on the running board of the car are, from left to right, June Woodruff; her son John Woodruff; her husband, John VanZandt Woodruff; and Miles Woodruff and Kathryn Woodruff, who are parents of John VanZandt Woodruff. The elder Woodruffs managed the inn from 1916 until 1947, when the business was sold to their son John VanZandt Woodruff, who ran it until 1961. (Courtesy of John and Wynne Woodruff.)

Ralph Brongo is holding his son Ralph T. Brongo on his shoulders while vacationing at Conesus Lake during the summer of 1952. Ralph was the owner of a building and development company located in Gates, New York. The family rented from Mary Coccia for several years before purchasing a cottage on McPherson Point in 1963. (Courtesy of Ralph T. and Linda B. Brongo.)

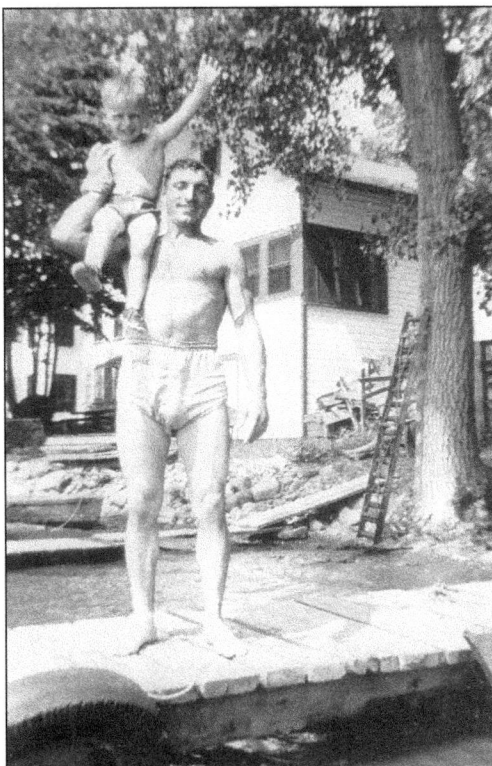

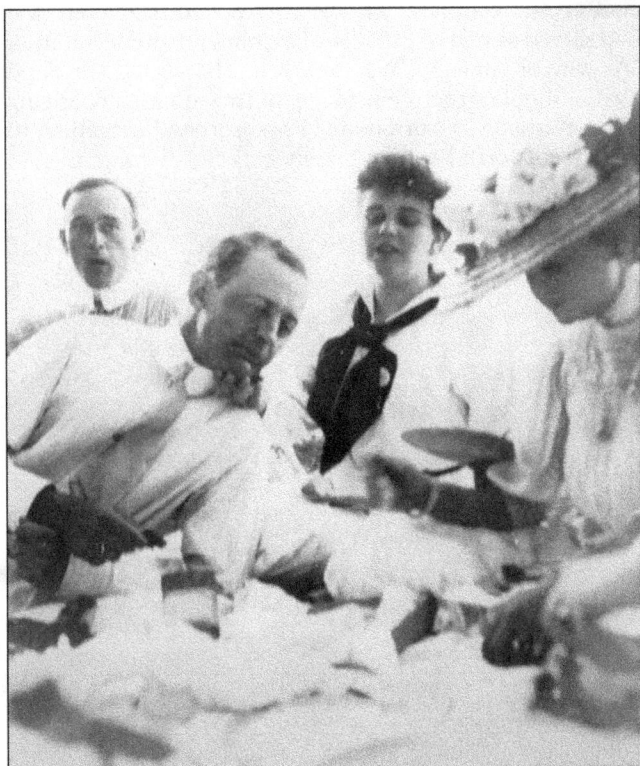

James Wolcott Wadsworth Jr., second from the left, is enjoying a picnic with unidentified family members in July 1908. He used the family cottage on Sand Point as a weekend getaway from his duties as a cattle rancher at the family homestead. The homestead was the Hartford House located in Geneseo, New York. At the time of this photograph, he was representing Livingston County as a New York State assemblyman. He would continue on in politics to become a US senator. (Courtesy of Harry R. Wadsworth.)

Alice Hay Wadsworth, whose father had served as one of President Lincoln's private secretaries, poses at Conesus Lake in July 1908. As wife of James W. Wadsworth Jr., she visited the Sand Point cottage frequently. The cottage was a simple structure made up of two rooms, a changing area in the front, and a bedroom in the back that was "surrounded by poison ivy," according to Harry Wadsworth. (Courtesy of Harry R. Wadsworth.)

During the summer of 1944, gas was rationed due to World War II. These girls were lucky enough to know someone with a car and gas rations to drop them off for a week of vacation near Eagle Point. The rental included a rowboat, while groceries were purchased at Sackett's Harbor. Dressed up to walk to church are, from left to right, Elvita Cimino, Ann Amico, Mary Capozzi, and Dolly Guarino. (Courtesy of Philip M. Mistretta.)

Earl Evans (left) and Chester "Chet" Cooligan (right) are sitting on the wharf at the hamlet of Van Valkenburg on July 6, 1915. The two cousins took a post-holiday canoe trip that began in the outlet at Lakeville, continued along the west side of the lake, and ended at Van Valkenburg. The posts of the dock that the steamships had used were still visible in that area up until just a few years ago. (Courtesy of Dorothy Ann Lush Liberati.)

# Five

# HOTELS AND INNS

The Iroquois Inn was located on the west side of the lake on what was then known as Iroquois Point. Situated between the areas of Cottonwood and Maple Beach, the inn was the former Butterways cottage. Eugene Sutton, proprietor, purchased the property about 1898 from a Geneseo businessman and operated it as a summer rental.

Phil Farley took over operation of the Excelsior Springs Hotel during the 1934 summer season. As Prohibition had just ended the year before, it was advertised as having "all legal beverages." Originally named for the sulpher springs located on the property, the hotel took on the Farley name as Hotel Farley or just Farley's. Long after the passing of the proprietor, it is still known today as The Farley apartments on East Lake Road. (Courtesy of the Livingston County Historians Office.)

Pictured in the 1930s is the shoreline of the Excelsior Springs Hotel. Several boats and a chair swing were available for use by hotel guests. This area is still open to the public today for use by guests of the Conesus Lake Campground. The campground has occupied this area since 1962.

74

In 1937, Fetzners Tavern operated out of this building at 2170 East Lake Road. Joseph Scardilla took over management in 1964. He had placed a simple sign by the road with the word "Conesus" on the image of a martini glass with reflective markers to attract customers, until the name was officially changed to Conesus Inn. Patrons could follow the sidewalk with the iron rail and enter a small bar to order a drink or a sandwich. His specialty was ham or roast beef sandwiches stuffed two inches thick for $1. (Courtesy of the Livingston County Historians Office.)

Joe Scardilla built up the reputation of the restaurant from a bar that served sandwiches to a fine dining establishment known throughout the country. The Scardilla family ran the Conesus Inn for 48 years with management passing from Joe to his son Roy and family. Chef Don Carll served the last meal in December 2012. The building was sold in the fall of 2013.

Pictured here in August 2010, the bar area at the Conesus Inn was styled like an old-time hotel, and balcony facade with dozens of antiques surrounded the bar area. The stained-glass window was retrieved from a church in Wayland by Roy Scardilla, who waded through mounds of pigeon droppings to get to the gem. (Courtesy of Judy Mistretta Patti.)

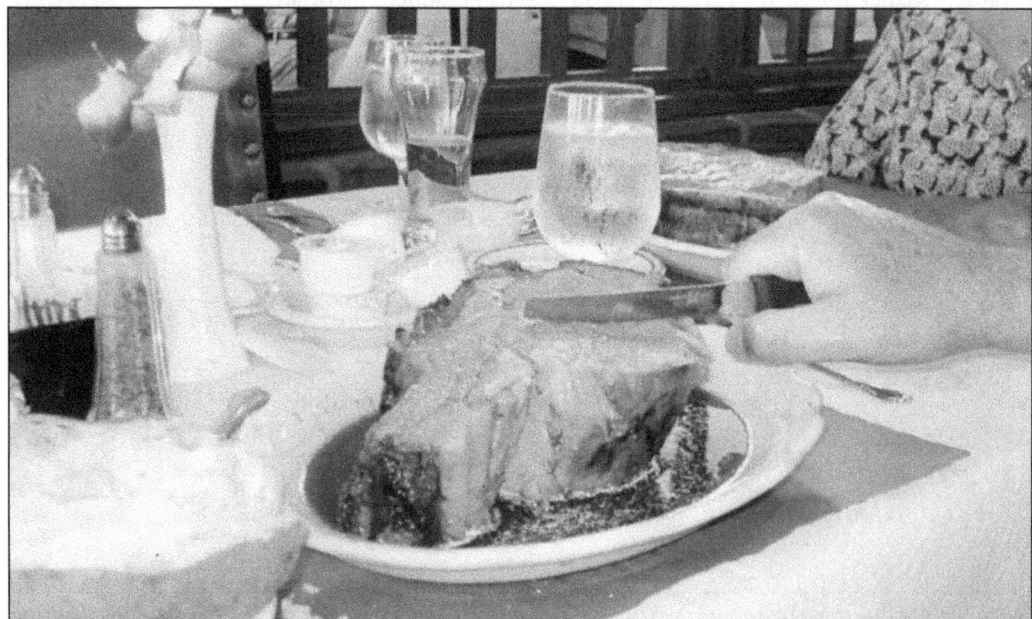

"For the Prime of Your Life" was the motto of the Conesus Inn. Slow-roasted and carved to order, prime rib was the signature meal of the inn. Four different cuts were available to order, the princess, queen, king, or truman, as well as a full menu. This was the king cut. (Courtesy of Judy Mistretta Patti)

The Van Valkenburg Hotel, pictured here about 1880, was a summer resort on the west side of the lake. Hotel guests were delivered by steamboat to a lake wharf. Orrin Van Valkenburg was the original landowner and proprietor of the hotel for 40 years. It was totally destroyed by fire in March 1913, a defective chimney the suspected cause. (Courtesy of the Livingston County Historians Office.)

Not to be confused with the Cottonwood Inn of the late 20th century located on Cottonwood Point, the original Cottonwood Inn opened for the first season in May 1921, in the rebuilt Van Valkenburg Hotel, under the operation of Carl R. Fedder of Dansville, New York. It could only be reached by a dirt road. In 1931, the county proposed to move West Lake Road 1,100 feet closer to the building. Fedder created quite a stir claiming $20,000 in damages as the move would disturb the quiet of his sleeping porches. The porches, the inn's signature feature, can be seen on the second floor. (Courtesy of the Livingston County Historians Office.)

The county won, and the road was moved up the hill from the lake. B. "Bert" Yawman and his wife, Anna, then purchased the Cottonwood in 1938. The couple enclosed the porches for dining, installed the newest of venetian blinds, and changed the name to Yawman's Tavern. The new owners sponsored bowling leagues, held banquets, and hosted clambakes that drew crowds from all over Western New York. It was sold in 1950 and renamed the Pink Elephant. (Courtesy of the Livingston County Historians Office.)

Bob Corris opened the Beachcomber Restaurant in May 1953 in the former Peg's Point grocery store. He removed the roadside gas pumps and remodeled the entire building with a beach-island theme. The store was replaced with small motel rooms, which had balconies built off the back of the building that faced the water.

John DeLucca built the original fireplace in the dining room of the Beachcomber using stone from the southern end of the lake. It had seashells stuck on it to go along with the island theme. Today, the current owners carry on the theme with seashell-decorated tables. DeLucca also built the fireplace at the Welch farm in Geneseo, the home of the family that delivered milk around the lake.

The restaurant part of the Beachcomber was completed at lake level and included a gift shop and a dining room with a wall of windows that allowed a view of the lake while enjoying a meal. To add more to the theme, sand was tossed about the floor. Above the bar, there was a large thatched-like roof with a cage behind it that held 25 parakeets, plus a parrot in his own cage. Outside umbrella-shaded tables and artificial palm trees lined the beach. The Beachcomber "set the pace for Resort Elegance," according to advertisements.

The Beachcomber Restaurant is seen as it looked in 1961. Paul and Eleanor Kiedrowski were the owners at the time with Paul as the chef and Eleanor as the baker. Advertisements touted it as "Western New York's most unusual year-round resort." Keeping with the South Seas island theme from the original owner, the artificial palm trees were left on the beach. Today, Thomas and Mary Alice May manage it. (Courtesy of the Livingston County Historians Office.)

Dr. James C. Jackson, who also managed the successful "Our Home on the Hillside" health resort in Dansville, owned property at Maple Beach in 1868. He was a firm believer of hydrotherapy or "water cure," which is the use of clean, pure water to cleanse the body of impurities. From time to time, he opened his lakeside home to the public for rest and rehabilitation. (Courtesy of Norman "Ron" and Nancy Anderson.)

The Maple Beach Inn was a summer resort created in 1890 from the former property of Dr. Jackson. A seasonal post office was opened at the inn in 1892. Pictured here in 1922, the resort sat on eight acres with over 1,000 feet of lakefront, groves of pine trees, and a well-groomed lawn that reached to the edge of the water. (Courtesy of Norman "Ron" and Nancy Anderson.)

The enormous size of the Livingston Inn can be seen from this hilltop photograph. Built in 1866, the inn was originally a sanitarium in the town of Avon and was known as the Avon Cure. William Strowger purchased it in 1904, tore it down piece-by-piece, and moved it to McPherson Point. The boards were numbered, shipped by rail to Lakeville, and then moved by boat to this location. (Courtesy of Norman "Ron" and Nancy Anderson.)

A simple sign marks the way to the Livingston Inn on McPherson Point. East Lake Road is the dirt road in the foreground. The road leading to the inn was called Lindsley Avenue at the turn of the 20th century. It has since been renamed McPherson Point Road. (Courtesy of Donald and Bernice Wolf Collection.)

Miles Woodruff purchased the Livingston Inn and surrounding park area on McPherson Point in 1916. The hotel was three stories high with an additional four-story section that could accommodate a total of 200 guests. Formal dress was worn to dinner. Together with his wife, Kathryn, and later his son John V. Woodruff with his wife, June, the family managed the hotel for 45 years. They sold it in 1961, the year of this picture. (Courtesy of the Livingston County Historians Office.)

The interior of a side room of the Livingston Inn shows the comfortable surroundings that were provided for hotel guests. In this room, guests could come to read a book, play cards, or simply be warmed by the fireplace. (Courtesy of John and Wynne Woodruff.)

The Livingston Inn had its own icehouse built on the premises. Employees cut blocks of ice just off the shoreline of McPherson Point and then they used horses to drag the blocks to the three-story icehouse. The ice was stored under sawdust until needed for use by the 80-room inn. (Courtesy of John and Wynne Woodruff.)

THE BIG TREE INN, McPherson Point, Conesus Lake.
FRANK AINSWORTH, Proprietor.

The Big Tree Inn was a second hotel on McPherson Point in the early 1900s. It was situated on a parcel of land adjacent to the Livingston Inn. Frank O'Conner of Geneseo owned the building, and leased it to H. Frank Ainsworth. In June 1908, Ainsworth extensively remodeled the hotel in order to accommodate more guests, including a 100-foot-long hitch shed for their horses. (Courtesy of the Livingston County Historians Office.)

H.F. AINSWORTH     BIG TREE INN     CONESUS LAKE, N.Y.

Ainsworth was proprietor of the Big Tree Inn until it closed in 1913. Ellery R. Bolles held an auction that year of the entire contents of the hotel, including the linoleum on the floor. Eventually, the new owner of the Livingston Inn, Miles Woodruff, tore down the building. Two small cottages and one larger cottage were built from the wood. (Courtesy of John and Wynne Woodruff.)

The Recreation Inn, seen at left in 1947, was a hotel and restaurant located on West Lake Road next to the Cottonwood Golf Course. It may have been the first establishment to offer the buy-one-get-one dinner deal, when in May 1954 the restaurant advertised the following in a local newspaper: "A Novel Dinner Deal—Two Dinners for the Price of One before 8 pm." Residents remember the lovely piano music offered on weekends by Mac McCumber or Chet Keely. (Courtesy of the Livingston County Historians Office.)

The Culver Manor Tearoom was a seasonal restaurant and hotel on the east side of Conesus Lake just south of Camp Stella Maris. The management offered dancing every night with an orchestra playing on the weekends. Pictured here in 1946, the three-story resort stood on a hill overlooking the water from 1911 until it was consumed by fire in 1964. (Courtesy of the Livingston County Historians Office.)

The card (shown upside-down in the image):

Sundays from 1 to 9 PM

Dinners Daily from 5 to 10 PM

BANQUETS, RECEPTIONS
PICNIC AREA
BOAT DOCKING AND BOAT LAUNCHING

Pictured above on a folding business card, Fisherman's Wharf was the last restaurant to operate on McPherson Point. It opened in May 1962 in the same area as the Livingston Inn and amusement park. The inn had been in disrepair and was torn down along with the park buildings the previous year. The interior of the new restaurant was designed to resemble an old Cape Cod fishing wharf and included a marina, boat launch, and a new clubhouse for the Conesus Lake Yacht Club. The restaurant was so successful that, two years later, overflow crowds were sent south to the newly opened Conesus Inn. Fisherman's Wharf operated until 1969, when it too was consumed by fire.

This image depicts a poster advertising Fisherman's Wharf. In 1979, the poster was found in between the walls while remodeling a house on McPherson Point.

The Tee n Gee Restaurant is located near the corner of East Lake Road and Big Tree Road in the hamlet of Lakeville. The location started out as a grocery store and gas station run by the LaHaye family in the 1930s. In the past, it has been called Mama's Place and Dot and Bill's Restaurant. The building has been a tavern of some sort for over 70 years.

The Pine Tree Manor on East Lake Road is pictured here from the south side in this undated photograph. Originally the homestead of the Long family of Livonia, it opened for the 19th season as a restaurant on May 29, 1940. A 1939 newspaper advertised the Pine Tree as a "Farm Home," serving food prepared from ingredients produced on its farm. (Courtesy of the Livingston County Historians Office.)

*Six*

# FLOODS, STORMS, AND SUCH

A St. Patrick's Day ice storm hit the Northeast on March 17, 1935. It lasted three days, leaving this house on McPherson Point and the town without electricity. Newspapers reported that roads were slushy and treacherous, but that "milk wagons were able to get through." Livonia firemen stood a 24-hour watch at the firehouse as the siren for emergencies was out of commission.

On March 3, 1991, a heavy, freezing rain caused loss of power all over Western and Northern New York. The local newspapers called it "the Great Ice Storm of '91." The Rochester and Finger Lakes areas were especially hard hit, affecting more than half a million people. Repair crews from as far away as Canada and Pennsylvania arrived to help restore power. These unidentified linemen are making repairs on East Lake Road.

The John Mooney residence in Lakeville was just east of the outlet on the park road. Pictured here in the rowboat navigating the floodwaters of March 1912 are, from left to right, Lloyd Bates, Paul Roe, and Earl Eddy. (Courtesy of the Livingston County Historians Office.)

The rushing water of a spring thaw could only be controlled by the throes of nature before formal regulation laws were put into place. Logjams and damage to the surrounding woods can be seen in this photograph taken of Conesus Lake around 1915. (Courtesy of the Village and Town of Geneseo.)

The cottages of the southern shore at Long Point were overtaken by floodwaters in 1956. The US Army Corps of Engineers now manages the flow of the outlet water, and the Conesus Lake Compact of Towns manages the lake level. (Courtesy of Norman "Ron" and Nancy Anderson.)

The flooded shoreline of the southern end of East Lake Road, part of the Excelsior Springs section of the lake, can be seen from the air in this 1972 photograph. The picnic tables and barns in the upper right corner are the beginnings of the Southern Shores Campground on the former Harper Day farm. (Courtesy of Mary Lee Cisco.)

An unidentified man and his dog are standing in the floodwaters that overtook Eagle Point on the west side of Conesus Lake in 1972. Hurricane Agnes formed on June 14 of that year over the Yucatan Peninsula, Mexico. It reached the lake on June 22 as a tropical storm. After raining for three days, the lake level reached its highest point ever at 822.50 feet above sea level on June 24, 1972. (Purchased from the collection of the Rochester Public Library Local History Division)

These cottages on Long Point were just one of the low-lying areas of the lake that were hit the hardest. It was estimated that the lake rose four feet from the rains of Tropical Storm Agnes, an amount equal to a total of 4.6 billion gallons of water. This flood is considered one of the greatest natural disasters in Genesee Valley history. (Purchased from the collection of the Rochester Public Library Local History Division.)

Conesus has seen its share of accidents, but this one had a positive outcome. An experimental plane crashed in the lake between Long Point and McPherson Point in 1986. Divers were called to assist in bringing the aircraft to shore. It was taken out at the New York State Boat Launch on East Lake Road, Livonia. Lake residents gathered at the launch and went out in their boats to help if needed. The pilot survived, as did the light aircraft. The Federal Aviation Administration shows that the N number of this plane has been reassigned to an airplane in Arizona. (Both, courtesy of John A. "Cubby" Rhode Jr.)

# Seven

# AMUSEMENTS AND RECREATION

Conesus Drive-In Theatre opened in July 1956. It was built in the hamlet of Lakeville on 15 acres of farmland, previously owned by Homer Benson. The huge screen was 150 feet long and 68 feet high. According to local newspaper reports, it was a modern RCA screen that was only the fourth installation in the United States at that time.

Located at the corner of Bronson Hill Road and Routes 15 and 20A, the Conesus Drive-In had room for 600 cars. On weekends during the summer, cars would line the roadside to purchase tickets before the gates were even open. Because Bronson Hill Road ran behind the drive-in, a few pranksters would walk in through the bushes that lined the road to avoid the price of admission. Despite this problem, the drive-in remained in business for 30 years.

In 1961, the Lima Baptist Church sponsored church on Sunday mornings at the drive-in. On Saturdays, during the mid-1970s, a flea market was held on the grounds. The Conesus Drive-In closed at the end of the 1986 season. A developer from Mendon, New York, purchased the property and created a business park at the location. The local fire department assisted with a controlled burn of the concession stand.

98

The movie *Kelly's Heroes* was released in July 1970. It was shown at the Conesus Drive-In just two months later on September 6, 1970. This original poster was found in excellent condition inside the lake house of one of the last owners of the drive-in when it was sold in October 2011. (Courtesy of Robert Carll.)

Every year since 1981, the New York State Festival of Balloons has been held on Labor Day weekend in the town of Dansville, south of the lake. In 1986, this balloon hovered dangerously close to the water off Walkley's Landing. Several boaters rushed out to help. Thankfully, a rescue was not needed. (Courtesy of Ruth Beil Rhode.)

An 18-hole miniature golf course was part of an amusement park on McPherson Point that was located near the Livingston Inn. Miles Woodruff managed the five-acre park while his wife managed the inn. The golf course drew such large crowds that people would sometimes be standing in line at 2:00 in the morning waiting to play the game and would have to be turned away. (Courtesy of John and Wynne Woodruff.)

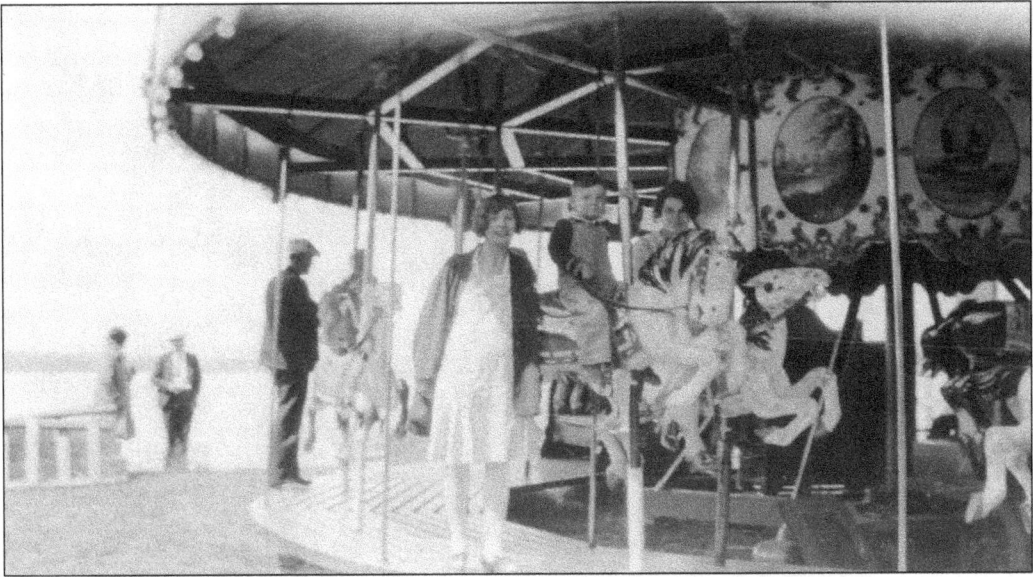

In addition to an amusement arcade with a shooting gallery, five skee ball alleys, darts, and a ring toss game, there was also a merry-go-round on the north side of the McPherson Point Park. A baseball diamond was on the acreage with a restaurant that sold hot dogs and popcorn to spectators. (Courtesy of John and Wynne Woodruff.)

These families are enjoying the water at McPherson Point around 1892. Pictured are members of two Bascom families, the Ben Morgan family, another Morgan family, and the Hixson family. Relaxing on the porch and bathing in the lake were favorite pastimes of vacationers in the 19th century. (Courtesy of the Livingston County Historians Office.)

These unidentified ladies are enjoying a hayride around 1892. They are part of a group of cottagers from McPherson Point. The residents would follow the baseball team that was based on McPherson Point to its weekly games. They would rent a "hayrack" and would travel together to cheer on their team. (Courtesy of the Livingston County Historians Office.)

The Mardi Gras Orchestra played at the dance hall in Long Point Park during the 1920s. Howard Gallagher is pictured in the center with his violin at his side. He and the other unidentified members of the orchestra were students of the college in Geneseo, New York. The popular orchestra also could be heard on the Rochester radio station WHAM. (Courtesy of Nancy Gallagher Monahan.)

The land that Long Point Park is on originally belonged to Geneseo landowner James Wadsworth. In the late 1800s, the family dedicated the park as a picnic area under the trees for all to enjoy. The area became a popular place for church picnics, Sunday strolls, and a place for families to gather by the lakeside.

Early parks were more like gardens where families could dress in their nicest clothes and spend a leisurely day together. Canoeing on the lake and strolls were the order of the day. (Courtesy of Norman "Ron" and Nancy Anderson.)

A bathhouse was built at the water's edge around the turn of the 20th century at Long Point Park, about the same time an amusement ride was being created known as the toboggan slide. This postcard, postmarked 1908, shows the bathhouse next to the toboggan slide at Long Point, so that the brave souls who rode the coasters into the water had a place to change. (Courtesy of Norman "Ron" and Nancy Anderson.)

Outdoor picnics originated as mobile outdoor meals enjoyed only by the wealthy. These ladies are enjoying a boxed lunch at Long Point in the summer of 1920. The affordability of the automobile helped to make these events available to the general public. Newspaper articles and books were written instructing the reader on how and where to have a picnic. Instructions such as "pure water should be nearby" and the "freedom from tormenting insect life" were given. (Courtesy of Norman "Ron" and Nancy Anderson.)

The park was open from Memorial Day to Labor Day. The dance hall on the right was built in 1923, and dancing was held nightly to an orchestra. Round and square dances were also provided. In 1936, a weekly beauty contest was held with the crowning of Miss Long Point at the end of the summer. (Courtesy of Norman "Ron" and Nancy Anderson.)

Harry and Margaret Berry managed Long Point Park for a total of 42 years. They are pictured in the second row along with other unidentified members of the park crew of 1933. He is wearing a suit, and she is seated to his left. (Courtesy of Walter Kingston Jr., Long Point Museum and Information Center.)

The Beer Tent was added to the park under the management of the Berry couple. In 1934, it was a true tent with sides that could be rolled down during inclement weather. Although changes were made to the tent in following years, the locals forever called it the "Beer Tent" at Long Point. (Courtesy of the Livingston County Historians Office.)

The Beer Tent was eventually modernized with a wooden pavilion-type roof and even a fireplace. However, the same tables and chairs were used until a 1988 fire brought the demise of the amusement park. They were part of the auction at the park in 1990. (Courtesy of Walter Kingston Jr., Long Point Museum and Information Center.)

The *Islander* tour boat was brought to Conesus Lake for the summer of 1926 from the Thousand Island area in Upstate New York. Purchased by Herbert DeGarmo for $6,000, it could travel at speeds up to 20 miles an hour. It had been quite a famous cruiser in the islands and sported wooden trim made of mahogany with wicker chairs for the tourists. (Courtesy of Norman "Ron" and Nancy Anderson.)

There was a high-flying trapeze act offered at Long Point Park during the 1940s. Longtime manager Carl Johnston married one of the performers, Charlotte, after he returned from World War II and took a job at Long Point. (Courtesy of Norman "Ron" and Nancy Anderson.)

The large summer crowds of beachgoers prompted a safety concern with Harry Berry, proprietor of Long Point Park, and in 1937, he established a lifesaving station. Trained lifeguards under the direction of chief lifeguard Howard Duffy of Geneva, New York, kept a constant presence at Long Point beach. Lessons in lifesaving and swimming were offered during the week at no charge to anyone who wanted to participate. (Courtesy of Norman "Ron" and Nancy Anderson.)

Here, the park at Long Point is all closed up for the winter of 1942. The arched-roof building on the right is the skating rink. Initially used as a dance hall, after World War II, it became a skating rink. In February 1958, the roof collapsed under the weight of heavy snow but was rebuilt by the summer season. (Courtesy of Norman "Ron" and Nancy Anderson.)

The building on the left was the penny arcade. The back of the arcade building was used in the 1950s to show Laurel and Hardy movies. A fire in the summer of 1988 completely destroyed both of these buildings, and in 1990, after an auction of the rides and equipment, the amusement park was closed for good. (Courtesy of Norman "Ron" and Nancy Anderson.)

This collection of memorabilia from the park includes, from left to right clockwise, coupons, which were given away to patrons who played a game; a ticket for the rides; a coin token; a matchbook cover; and an early pinback. Newspapers also advertised that a Packard car would be given away on Labor Day. (Courtesy of Norman "Ron" and Nancy Anderson; coin token courtesy of Sharon L. Mistretta.)

Ellen Trescott is riding in the *Roosevelt* at the Long Point Park boat ride about 1983. At that time, the rides were owned and operated by John and Alice LaGrou. The cottage that the family stayed in during the summer is behind the boat ride. Today, the caretaker's cottage is a museum that is operated by the Town of Geneseo, New York. The *Roosevelt* is on display in the museum. (Courtesy of Jim Trescott.)

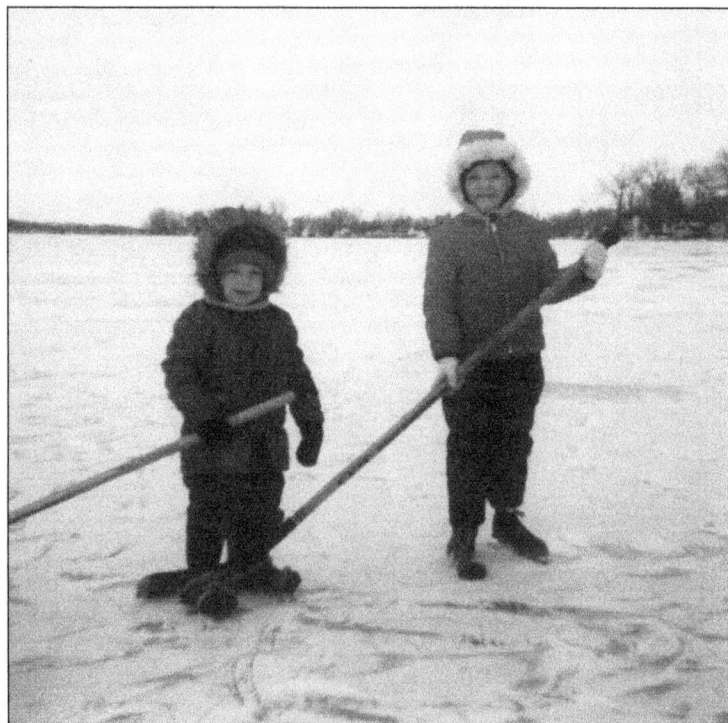

David Brongo Jr. (left) and Robbin Brongo (right) are practicing ice hockey off the shore of McPherson Point in 1976. The south side of Old Orchard Point can be seen in the distance. Each year, families all around the lake clear ice rinks for different winter sports.

Ice-skating is a favorite wintertime sport that has been enjoyed for years on the lake. Skating on Conesus Lake during the winter of 1926 are, from left to right, Jim ?, Jackie MacArthur, and unidentified. Jackie was the grandniece of Elizabeth Struble, who was housekeeper and caretaker at Sunnyside farm. (Courtesy of Mary Lee Cisco.)

Pictured sitting in a canoe in this photograph, taken in 1937, are Jack Williams (left) and Eleanor Williams (right). They are the children of Charles Williams and Myrtle Sutton. Charles was a local photographer of Conesus Lake; his photographs were then printed into postcards for tourists.

From left to right are a Mrs. Huck at the oars, Clara Dunspeck, Mildred Cooligan, and Betty Huck around 1924 at Lakeville. Leisurely rides in a rowboat or canoe were a favorite recreation in the early 1900s. (Courtesy of Dorothy Ann Lush Liberati.)

John A. "Cubby" Rhode Jr. is practicing slalom skiing near Dacola Shores at the southern end of the lake in May 1982. Practice times were early morning before school. The Beachcomber Ski Club had set out a course in that area for use by water-skiing enthusiasts, complete with a ramp for jumping. Membership in the club was not required for use of the course. (Courtesy of John A. "Cubby" Rhode Jr.)

*Eight*

# BUSINESSES

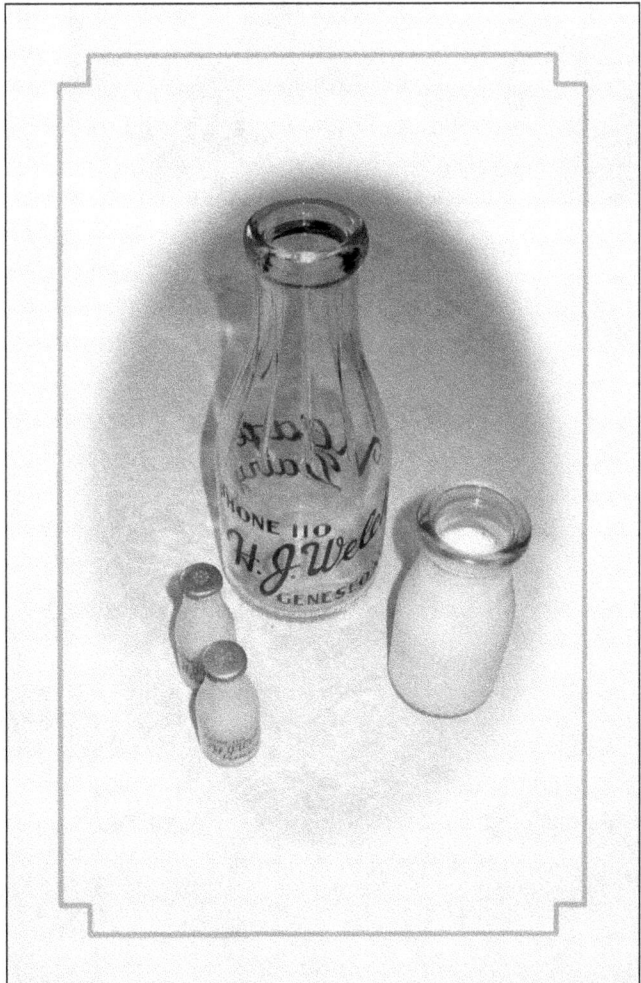

H.J. Welch Dairy was located on Lima Road in the town of Geneseo. Jerry Welch, also of Geneseo, was deliveryman. The dairy was established in 1913 and delivered milk to lake residents in three towns, Geneseo, Groveland, and Conesus, for nearly half a century. It was sold to Geneseo Dairies, Inc., in 1951. (Courtesy of Polly Camp.)

A post office was built in the hamlet of Van Valkenburg across from the hotel of the same name. Orrin Van Valkenburg was instrumental in establishing the post office and served as the first postmaster. In 1898, a Mr. Masten and his team of horses, known as the Floyd McNinch team, delivered the mail from the town of Conesus via Maple Beach.

The building that now houses just the Lakeville Liquor Store was the home of several businesses in the 1960s. George Russell Real Estate office was in the back of the building while the liquor store was in front and was operated by George's wife, Helen. Sal Joy of Rochester opened a barbershop on the left side in July 1960. The right side was the first office of J. Michael Jones, a well-known Geneseo attorney. (Courtesy of Robyn Price.)

Looking north on East Lake Road in the photograph above, at the entrance to McPherson Point, was Tompkins Grocery, situated on the curve. Eva Tompkins is pictured on the steps to the left of the house in the photograph below. She and her husband, Norman, operated the store in 1925. In addition to chocolates and ice cream, as the signs on the store advertise, the owners stocked and carried all the necessary items for cottagers and residents alike. Lyle and Alta Searles ran the store during the 1960s and into the early 1970s. They expanded service to include a dock and gas pumps for boaters, employing local teens to pump the gas. Their living quarters occupied half of the house, and they could often be seen when one stood at the counter waiting for service, in their own rockers, gazing out the picture window watching the waves and waiting for customers.

McPHERSON POINT GROCERY                              CONESUS LAKE

Archibald "Archie" MacArthur was an East Lake Road resident and a house mover by trade. He had moved big barns and a house in Fairport during his career. An unidentified member of his crew prepares a lakeside building for transport in this 1959 photograph. The entire family participated in some moves, with his wife, Jackie, and daughter Mary Lee flagging traffic, while his son Douglas assisted with the heavier work. (Courtesy of John MacArthur.)

The first water move for the MacArthur crew came along in May 1964, when they floated a cottage in sections about a mile across Conesus Lake. The cottage belonged to George Beach of East Lake Road in the Sunny Shores section and was sold to Joseph Curran on West Lake Road in the Wadsworth Cove section. The living room encountered strong winds near McPherson Point and was grounded overnight. Pranksters put a flag on the roof with skull and crossbones and the words "Mack the Mover." (Courtesy of John MacArthur.)

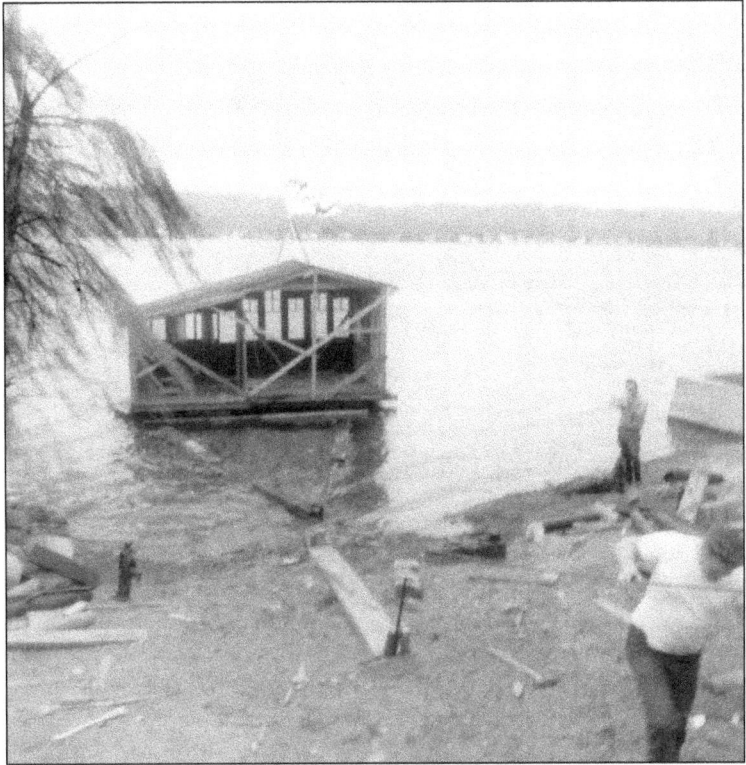

John MacArthur, brother of house mover Arch MacArthur, and his unidentified helper pull the living room section of a cottage to its new home. Another section of living room, a sleeping porch, and a bathroom were all moved by water. (Courtesy of John MacArthur.)

The Cottonwood Golf Course opened August 1926, with the backing of Frederick A. Owen of Dansville, New York. There were two courses consisting of a nine-hole course above another nine-hole approach course used for putting and warming up. The entire area sat 200 feet above the water, sparking jokes that a golfer could get dizzy at the tee. A weekday round of golf cost 75¢. (Courtesy of Livingston County Historical Society.)

The Cottonwood Golf Course attracted hundreds of golfers through the 1930s. In 1941, a tearoom was opened in the clubhouse. However, by the 1950s, interest waned in the steep-climbing course, and the property was abandoned. A former star pitcher for the New York Yankees, Vic Raschi, bought the acreage in 1957 for his private home. (Courtesy of the Livingston County Historians Office.)

Spencer Tooey, nicknamed "Colonel Tooey," operated a boat sales and service business south of Long Point Park for over 50 years. The sales office stocked everything needed for boating or canoeing, as well as gifts and mementos of Conesus Lake. He also offered rides in one of his speedboats with special rates for people who were picnicking at Long Point. (Courtesy of the Village and Town of Geneseo.)

Colonel Tooey is at the helm of one of several speedboats that he owned and operated out of his marina on the lake. Tooey was a businessman in two states. He operated Silver Springs Jungle Cruise in Florida as well as his business on Conesus. To promote sales of his boats, he often brought performers from Florida to New York for publicity stunts. (Courtesy of the Livingston County Historians Office.)

The Tooey gang is seen about 1937. Pictured are, from left to right, (sitting) Jerry Tooey; (standing) Colonel Tooey; Dr. Robert Dublin of Rochester, New York; Leo "Mac" McGuire; Dr. Theodore Martens of Rochester, Minnesota; Lucille Vogt of Ocala, Florida; and George Taylor. (Courtesy of the Livingston County Historians Office.)

These Tooey boats were excursion boats used by Colonel Tooey. A price of 50¢ would get the rider a tour around the shoreline of the lake. Colonel Tooey would sit at the back of the boat and point out areas of special interest. He kept the boats at the Long Point dock as his headquarters was nearby. (Courtesy of Norman "Ron" and Nancy Anderson.)

The *Islander* tour boat is docked at McPherson Point as the unidentified members of its crew lean on the stern. Colonel Tooey is piloting one of his speedboats on the return trip to the Long Point dock. He ran a livery service between Long Point and McPherson Point, charging the customer just 10¢ a trip. (Courtesy of John and Wynne Woodruff.)

Colonel Tooey, not only owned the *Riot*, but also the *Rocket*, the *Hyball*, the *Flash*, and the *Thunderbolt*. He boasted that speeds up to 50 miles per hour could be reached by some of his boats. (Courtesy of the Livingston County Historians Office.)

Owner Walter "Red" VanIngen is seen standing on the steps of the Lakeville Inn at the corner of Route 15 and Stone Hill Road about 1948. This historic inn began as a tavern and stagecoach stop. The inn was thought to be over 100 years old when it was destroyed by fire in 1950. (Courtesy of Livonia Preservation and Historical Society.)

LEN SACKETT
GENERAL STORE

"SACKETT'S HARBOR, CONESUS LAKE"

The Sackett's Harbor grocery was a busy place during the 1930s. Managed by L.M. Sackett, the store was located just south of Eagle Point. In addition to groceries, there were gas pumps, boat livery, camping and picnic grounds, and cottage rentals. Just in case a patron wanted to own a cottage instead of rent one, L.M. Sackett was also a licensed real estate broker, who could handle the sale. (Courtesy of Norman "Ron" and Nancy Anderson.)

Hundreds of spectators gather at the shore of Long Point Park to get a look at a flying boat. Both Thomas Brothers of Ithaca and Glenn Curtiss of Hammondsport were building this type of aircraft; however, Thomas Brothers was the first to construct the hull out of metal instead of wood. They produced the boats from 1912 to 1915. (Courtesy of Norman "Ron" and Nancy Anderson.)

122

The Thomas Brothers Aeroplane Company of Bath, New York, ran a flying school off McPherson Point in 1913. Included among the several aviators conducting lessons for the school was Walter E. Johnson, an exhibition pilot for the company. Tuition was $250 per week.

In 1914, Johnson incorporated his own flying school with partner C.A. Herman, the Walter E. Johnson School of Aviation at Livonia, New York. He operated out of the Livingston Inn. It was advertised as "a school for water flying machines" and used a hydroplane and a flying boat, built by the Thomas Brothers Company.

A young pilot lost his life in August 1915 while flying with the Johnson School near Orchard Point on the lake. Lawrence Lyon of Ithaca, who was 22 years old, lost control of his hydroplane and crashed unexpectedly into the lake. The Johnson School was closed shortly thereafter with a little over a year of operation. (Courtesy of Norman "Ron" and Nancy Anderson.)

The large building with a chute to the frozen water is the Lakeville Icehouse, photographed about 1915. Before refrigeration, ice blocks were cut from the lake for cooling foods at homes and businesses. Standing in the foreground to the right of the icehouse are, from left to right, C. Beach and Frank Yost. Almost 45,000 tons of ice could be stored in the building. (Courtesy of the Livingston County Historians Office.)

Ice Harvest at Conesus Lake, Lakeville, N. Y.

These teams from the Silver Lake Ice Company of Rochester are preparing to remove the snow from the ice. It was a two-step process involving horse-drawn scrapers to clear the snow and get down to the desirable clear ice. Both men and horse wore cork shoes to avoid slipping. (Courtesy of the Livingston County Historians Office.)

Ice harvest Conesus Lake, Lakeville, N. Y.

The Silver Lake Company employed 200 to 275 men at the icehouse in Lakeville. These men are using long poles to push the ice cakes through water canals that had been cut in the ice. The large cakes were as long as a yardstick and just as thick. The ice was then packed in sawdust to prevent melting. (Courtesy of Norman "Ron" and Nancy Anderson.)

These unidentified men are cutting ice from the lake in the winter of 1909. The cottages in the background belong to the families of Bender, Wesbury, McClintock, and Bertha Owen. The mild weather early in that year yielded a small ice crop, and by the end of February, the huge icehouse was only half full. (Courtesy of the Livingston County Historians Office.)

DOCK AND ICE HOUSE, CONESUS LAKE.                                    Livonia, N. Y.

The area of the Lakeville Icehouse was a much quieter place during the summer months with the absence of men and horses. However, shipment of the ice to customers continued through the end of the month of November. The cycle began all over again when temperatures dipped and ice formed again in January. (Courtesy of Norman "Ron" and Nancy Anderson.)

126

These unidentified employees of the Creamery at Lakeville are taking a lunch break. The milk condensing plant used 10,000 gallons of lake water per hour. The lakeside location and the proximity to the Erie Railroad tracks proved profitable for the company, allowing them to ship two railroad cars per day to major cities such as New York and Washington. (Courtesy of Norman "Ron" and Nancy Anderson.)

A 1941 Piper Cub Seaplane is preparing for a water landing on Conesus Lake. The Lux Marine that is advertised on the side of the seaplane was located on East Lake Road. Paul Lux owned the marina from 1957 to 1960. The location, however, has been an active marina for well over 60 years. (Courtesy of the Livingston County Historians Office.)

Visit us at
arcadiapublishing.com

www.ingramcontent.com/pod-product-compliance
Lightning Source LLC
Chambersburg PA
CBHW080615110426

42813CB00006B/1510